TEAM
for Actors

A Holistic Approach to Embodied Acting

TEAM
for Actors

A Holistic Approach to Embodied Acting

Laura Bond

TEAM
for Actors
A Holistic Approach to Embodied Acting
©2012 Laura Bond
www.teamforactors.com

Book Design by Janet Aiossa
Photography and Photo Illustration by Ron Morecraft
Posture Modeling by Katherine Palm and Robert Abrahamson

ISBN-13: 978-1-4792800-6-3
ISBN-10: 1-4792800-6-2

Printed in the USA

TEAM
for Actors

A Holistic Approach to Embodied Acting

Acknowledgements

I often tell acting students, "No actor is an island." I think it helps them understand that acting is a community engaged art form that cannot exist without the support of others. This consideration can be as simple as needing an audience to witness the work, or having actors act off other actors, creating an ensemble, and taking direction. Then there are the many individuals responsible for contributing to a performance piece as a whole: writers, designers, managers, run crews, marketing teams, facilities staff, etc.

I feel the same about my writing, and the process of creating this book. Without contributions and support of so many individuals over the years, this book would not be possible. I dedicate this book to two very influential groups of people who made this text feasible: (1) the group of students that embraced these ideas, exercises, and techniques in my acting classes and rehearsals, and whose experiences and stories are included in this book, and (2) my Asheville writers group who faithfully and tirelessly read, re-read, critiqued, encouraged and pushed me to find my voice on this subject during its seven years of development. To them, I will be forever grateful!

Special thanks to:

- UNC-Asheville for the ongoing support during the writing and development of this book and its techniques

- Asheville Writers' Group members: Barbara, Bonita, and Lavinia

- My family, friends, and dear husband, for their support and encouragement

- Dr. Susana Bloch, for her development of, and dedication to, expanding and sharing the Alba Emoting™ technique.

- Jack and Carole King, for offering their beautiful homes as writing retreats at the beginning stages of this book in the summer of 2005

- Stephanie Schlie, my editor, for her meticulous attention to detail, and honest appraisal of each chapter's clarity

Table of Contents

"A word does not start as a word—it is an end product which begins as an impulse, stimulated by attitude and behavior which dictate the need for expression."

– Peter Brook

Chapter 1

Introduction

TEAM for Actors: *A Holistic Approach to Embodied Acting*

Actors surround us with performances every day: on televisions, in movies, on phones and through computers. Actors sell products, report the news, and satirize current events. They entertain, inform, and entreat us into new experiences. Through performance, actors move us to think, feel, and behave differently. They convince us that we are watching reality, even when we are not. They enact the stories by novelists, playwrights, script writers, storytellers, poets, and song writers. We rely on actors to provide skilled performances. We want them to move us, to invite us to merge with their imaginary worlds. Actors are the conduits for all these vital theatrical experiences.

Highly skilled actors can woo their audiences into believing a fictionalized reality. These actors play their characterized parts without the audience recognizing that finely tuned skills were applied to their acting craft—so fine the acting technique is invisible. In other words, as Jimmy Stewart is known for saying, "It's well done if you can do a part and not have the acting show." Well done acting takes a great deal of skill, and yet is applied as if it were delivered effortlessly.

An actor's skill development is much like that of the magician's process for creating his magic on stage. A student magician studies, practices, and often fumbles through endless hours of preparation in order to make his conjuring appear swift and easy. He works long hours convincing fine muscles to carry out intricate moves. One hand flourishes to distract while the other secretly completes an act of deception. Meanwhile, his face expresses joy and ease—to create a mystical moment inspiring awe from his audience.

In essence, students of acting are no different from those studying to be magicians. Acting students also use their entire bodies to prepare for a role, and they are highly dedicated to skill development and concentrated practice. Magicians' intentions may be to dazzle, the actors' skills are hidden behind characters who are often as common as you or I. In such cases their talents and skills become invisible. The actor may not appear as awe-inspiring as the magician, whose performance is so foreign to a common life. Great acting skills are often so well integrated into the resulting performance that the actual skill behind that performance can go unrecognized, unappreciated, and unfortunately, unknown to aspiring actors who need to recognize and value these skills the most.

When the actor successfully portrays a believable character, he manages to make the audience accept that the illusion he creates is reality. Peter Brook summarizes this point well in a passage from *The Empty Space*:

> *"The vehicle of drama is flesh and blood and here completely different laws are at work....A ballet dancer is sometimes close to this by his own personality or by the outer movement of life. But the moment the actor dresses up and speaks with his own tongue he is entering the fluctuating territory of manifestation and existence that he shares with the spectator."* [1]

An actor who manifests this kind of performance, regardless of the size of the role or the style of venue, is producing high quality, embodied acting.

Embodied Acting

The original meaning of the word *embody* was, "a soul or spirit invested with a physical form; of principles, ideas, etc." The word *embody* emerged from *en-body*, or to be "in-body."[2] Embodied acting is to give tangible, bodily, or concrete form to the abstract concepts revealed through scripts and stories. Fully embodied acting portrays all facets of a character's internal thoughts and feelings, as well as external actions, and shares them in truthful, believable human behavior. Embodied acting is necessary in productions from stage to

---

1. Peter Brook, *The Empty Space* (New York: Penguin Press, 1968), 17.
2. "Dictionary.com," accessed September 1, 2012, http://dictionary.reference.com.

television, to the big screen.

Renowned acting teachers like Stanislavski, Meisner, Hagen and Chekhov refer to embodiment techniques by stressing the study of the character's motivations as well as their resulting actions, or behavior. Sanford Meisner is known for displaying a framed sign hung in his New York City acting studio stating, "An Ounce of BEHAVIOR is Worth a Pound of WORDS."[3] Michael Chekhov's key Psychological Gestures are built upon the combination of thoughts (or Images), feelings, and will-impulses (or actions).[4] Uta Hagen describes detailed activity and sensory exercises for acting preparation. Stanislavski's acting books refer to embodiment techniques discussing action, imagination, objectives, emotion memory, and plasticity of motion. The basic theories of these respected teachers reflect a common message for actors. The ultimate goal of any actor is to perfect the study and portrayal of all facets of human behavior. However, far too many don't know how to manifest these theories into practice, and produce fully embodied acting. TEAM for Actors recognizes the benefits of many respected acting theories, and yet provides tangible, reliable tools that assist the actor in synthesizing theories into behavior that is supportive of the character's needs and desires.

Common Acting Techniques

Some acting techniques may only address one area of either the mental, physical, or emotional influences on behavior. People recognizing commonalities in these techniques categorize them under three general areas: (1) Inside-Out, (2) Outside-In, and (3) Emotion-Based.

The "Inside-Out" approach focuses on back-story and analysis. This technique suggests if the actor understands the character's history and way of thinking, the emotional and physical aspects will follow naturally. This theory might break down all the intricacies of the character's thoughts, past experiences, and future desires—but how do the characters feel about these desires, and then how do they show it? Using only this approach, the actor may not learn to connect her thoughts with actions and emotions. Actors who don't make holistic connections are often described as "talking heads" or "heady actors."

3. Sanford Meisner and Dennis Longwell, *Sanford Meisner On Acting* (New York: Vintage Books,1987), 4.
4. Michael Chekhov, *On the Technique of Acting* (New York: Routledge, 2003), 63.

Their performances can come off as stiff, closed in, and disconnected from the rest of their bodies, as well as from other actors.

The "Outside-In" approach proposes to "play the action." It suggests if the actor starts with a physical action or gesture it will provoke the inner life of thoughts and emotions to emerge. This technique focuses on the physical intricacies of muscles, breathing, movement, gesture, and activity. If the inner life of thoughts and needs does not connect with these movements we might ask, "Why is the character doing these actions, and how is he moved to do so?" Such actors are mesmerizing to watch, but the audience witnessing these acrobatics may be left searching for the character's motivations.

Emotion-Based acting approaches center around detailed emotional exploration. Some techniques in this category encourage the actor to connect with life experiences to evoke emotions similar to those of the character's situation. The techniques that consistently use the actor's traumatic life experiences to motivate their work can be very damaging to the psychological and emotional well-being of the actor. Performances based only in strong emotional behavior can be very moving to witness, but then, why is the character emotional, and how does she convey what she wants through behavior? Shakespeare might describe such performances as, "full of sound and fury, signifying nothing." Actors who learn a purely emotional approach and have not gained the skills in understanding character motivations or shifting beats of action, can come across as self-involved and inflexible.

Each of these techniques provides important tools for actors, and if looked upon as one of many approaches for the actor to study, each can become a valuable acting tool in the actor's "tool box." However, if an actor studies only one of these methods, she may miss the vital whole of her character, and her acting craft.

A Holistic Approach

The actor must always remain aware that in order to depict the entirety of human behavior, all parts that make the whole of being human must be studied and practiced. We are beings that think, feel, and behave as we manifest our lives. Acting is a living art, combining the current life of the actor with the imagined life of the character. There is a saying, "You cannot step into the same river twice," for not only is the river ever flowing and changing, but so are you. When an actor performs she intertwines the character with her own vibrant living system. Performing a character is a multi-layered process with two personalities interwoven in the act of presenting one.

An actor is responsible for creating a well-rounded truthful character who interacts with external conditions—the story, environment, and other characters and actors. At the same time the actor interacts with internal conditions—thoughts, emotions, and beliefs of the character and the actor. The actor must be constantly aware of the ever changing circumstances for the character <u>and</u> for the actor—both internally and externally. Every change and shift in these parts will affect the whole.

When we consider how complex this process is, we cannot simply rely on one aspect of this intricate whole. The actor needs a process that helps her explore all external and internal components, understand their inter-relationships, and learn the skills to connect these with her entire thinking, feeling, and being. *TEAM for Actors* provides this process.

TEAM for Actors

I developed *TEAM for Actors* while teaching for the University of North Carolina, Asheville Drama Department and as an international workshop instructor of Alba Emoting™. Since my arrival at UNCA in 1998 I recognized that student actors struggled with creating fully embodied acting. They often expressed an inability to grasp the concepts of creating clear active objectives based in strong needs and desires. They needed tangible techniques for selecting and embodying authentic and diverse expressions of their character's behavior. These students struggled most with putting all these elements together into a holistic product, as they favored one aspect of emotion, action, or intellectual investigation over the other. Their performances at the time could not manifest a full synthesis of these vital components in order to bring embodied life to the script. They did not realize that, as Peter Brook states so clearly, "A word does not start as a word—it is an end product which begins as an impulse, stimulated by attitude and behavior which dictate the need for expression."[5]

---

5. Peter Brook, *The Empty Space* (New York: Penguin Press, 1968), 40.

Actors who have not worked holistically may analyze the script for intellectual choices, but then leave these discoveries behind on the page and never fully connect those ideas to the final performance product. Or they make exciting emotional connections, yet do not fully understand why the character is so emotional. Another actor may have vigorous movements and gestures that fully embody a character, but lack either a grounding in the text or the application of subtle nuances that come from listening and reacting to another actor. It was through these discoveries and the need to provide actors with tools for making connections to all the aspects of an embodied performance that I created *TEAM for Actors*. I've thoroughly tested the approach, terms, and exercises in this book through extensive classroom and rehearsal investigation.

The TEAM

TEAM for Actors synthesizes three elements in human behavior: thought, emotion, and action. This holistic technique helps actors see how these three inter-related parts are present in the actor's life, in the character's life, and in basic human behavior. This union of the first three parts combined with the actor's Personal Connection to these elements manifests a fully realized, passionate, embodied performance.

TEAM is an acronym: Thought + **E**motion + **A**ction = **M**anifestation

The book provides a chapter for each aspect of the approach, presenting theories and tangible methods for exploring the areas of Thought, Emotion, and Action. The Manifestation chapter guides the actor through the process of unifying with the character's experience and moving from theory into embodiment.

TEAM for Actors unites: traditional actor training approaches, basic human behavior theory, and the somatic approach of Alba Emoting™. This unification assists the actor in moving from the theoretical, to the practical, and into the tangible. The root of the word *somatic* is *soma* meaning, "living body as experienced within," a term meant to resolve the gap between the mind and body, representing a holistic perspective of the person. This book often refers to the Alba Emoting™ technique[6], developed by neuroscientist Dr. Susana Bloch. Alba Emoting is a reliable, safe, and measurable method for embodying emotions and actions of expression. Alba Emoting theory is threaded throughout *TEAM for Actors* and provides a scientifically proven method for understanding and embodying expressive behavior. Alba Emoting offers a means for examining physiological activities, modes of expression, and the inner thoughtful experience of expressive behavior and how these elements then meld into a fully embodied performance.

The book includes many of my own original exercises created through years of experimenting with this approach. I also share stories of acting and directing experiences using *TEAM for Actors* in my classes and rehearsals. In order to connect these acting theories with basic human behavior, I include Maslow's basic psychological theory of a human hierarchy of needs and connect each term and method used in the TEAM to examples from daily life. Finally, since past acting teachers will always influence and inform the present, the book also refers to revered acting techniques, relevant terms, and traditional theories and exercises developed by notable acting teachers.

The TEAM as a Holistic Approach to Acting

Thoughts are intrinsically tied to emotions and actions, and these ultimately lead to manifested visible results. Some may call this result a performance, an act, living the part, living in one's words, or embodiment. Whatever name one assigns the result, *TEAM for Actors* makes it clear that all of these simultaneously cooperative elements create that result. These inter-related aspects are present in your life, in the character's life, and in all human behavior. When you feel an emotion, you simultaneously have thoughts about this emotion, or had thoughts that influenced that emotion. At the same time you engage behaviors and physical reactions to these thoughts and feelings. A multi-layered interactive communication process continues to build as you take actions that express additional emotions, develop reactive thoughts, and evoke these multiple layers in the behaviors of others.

[Example] A simple example of this from everyday life might be, when you express a hearty hello to someone, but they don't respond with a congenial hello back to you. You quickly develop your own thoughts about this exchange. Your

---

6. The trademark symbol for Alba Emoting is, from this point on, implied when referring to the technique.

thoughts then influence how you behave and then engage in further interactions with that person.

Since all these equally influential aspects are present in human behavior, *TEAM for Actors* addresses them as equal and reciprocal building blocks for creating quality acting. *TEAM for Actors* also recognizes that the resulting performance is the merging of actor and text. The actor analyzes and interprets text as a means of building a character that is supportive of the story. The Manifestation chapter includes methods for the actor to connect personally with the role, bringing the actor closer to believing in, and then embodying the character's situations.

Personal Use of the TEAM

The actor's personality, life history, and feelings about the character or the text all influence how she interprets the character. Likewise, the actor's style of learning, mode of receiving information, and personal preferences for physical, emotional, and intellectual engagement in the craft of acting will also influence her approach. Individual preferences for learning and developing a craft are important for an actor to recognize and respect. Additionally, an actor must acknowledge that the character she plays will also have these individual preferences for personal expression. So, the actor may play a character in one script that she feels is best to approach first from a physical angle and then fill in the other aspects of emotion and action. Yet, that same actor may play a role from another script where the character is highly intellectual and so requires a thought process first. Essentially the actor is recognizing her MVP (Most Valuable Player) of the TEAM. In sports terms, the MVP could be different for each game, and there may be a string of games where the same MVP was recognized as the most influential team member for each game. However, all team members contributed to the game, and all members were necessary. The same holds true for the TEAM in *TEAM for Actors*.

You may already know the MVP as your own acting style, your personal rehearsal process, or how you prefer to approach a role. One element of the TEAM can be used as a primary method of preparation for a specific type of role or style of play. It is vital for your growth as an actor to recognize your preferred use of individual parts of the TEAM, and how this preference may change from situation to situation. A versatile actor accepts that different approaches may be needed for varying styles of scripts and their characters. These are all examples of how you can use a part of the TEAM as an approach, or gateway into the acting work. However, eventually all elements of the TEAM need to be incorporated in order to provide a holistic product.

TEAM for Actors as a Companion Text

TEAM for Actors can also be used as a companion text with other acting techniques or embodiment methods. Although this text provides the groundwork for you to study the Alba Emoting technique as an embodiment method, other somatic approaches and many of the regarded acting techniques referred to in this text, would work well with the TEAM as an additional source for embodiment. You may also already have a favored method for embodiment, or may find that embodying comes easily by simply imagining the given circumstances. With this in mind, you may not need further study of other embodiment methods and may be able to employ the TEAM by using this text alone.

TEAM for Actors…and Directors

Whether you are an actor or director, once you understand how to apply this holistic approach to acting, you can easily recognize when acting is lacking the layers and dimensions necessary to present fully embodied, truthful behavior. *TEAM for Actors* offers building blocks for preparing any acting role, testing approaches to scene work, addressing the delivery of a song or dance, and preparing monologues. *TEAM for Actors* can also be used to deconstruct a performance. When a director observes a moment in rehearsal that is not coming across believably, the director can use a review of the TEAM to find the missing link. The side coaching techniques in this book also provide the director with rehearsal methods for coaching actors on elements of the TEAM and helping actors embody their choices in the moment. When acting, you can use the approach as a reflection method after receiving notes for changes from a director. Also, when you recognize that something is not working right in a scene or performance, you can use the TEAM as a review process before the next performance. Both actor and director can utilize the TEAM as an active tool for initially creating dynamic acting roles, and then as a retrospective analysis of performances in process.

How to Use This Book

I recommend that you read this entire book, while exploring all aspects of the TEAM. After doing so, you will be able to identify your own preferences for a TEAM MVP and learn how each element of the TEAM can be applied to varying roles, acting challenges, and script styles. Many acting students start my classes thinking they are partial to one element of the TEAM, but then after reading the text and engaging in the various chapter exercises, discover their preferences change. Often actors establish acting preferences based on habits or limited experience with other acting techniques. Once you are introduced to new approaches to scene study and character development, you will discover a fresh and more versatile process never before imagined.

This book provides clear steps within each part of the TEAM so that you can begin a rehearsal process by applying any one of the elements that make up the TEAM. By doing so, you are exploring how to use a specific TEAM entry point (or MVP) into the craft of acting and then learning how the other elements either emerge during rehearsals or need additional exercises provided by the text to bring all elements of the TEAM to the surface. In my acting classes we typically work on four different scenes throughout the semester, providing students with the opportunity to see what it is like to approach a scene with each of the elements of the TEAM, and to learn how and when the other remaining elements emerge during rehearsals. Using various MVPs as an approach to acting work acknowledges the varying needs for individual script styles and characters, as well as recognizes how each person has their own preferred mode of acting exploration. You may find that one element of the TEAM is more accessible to you, or to your character. You may struggle with one aspect while immediately understanding and fully engaging in the other. This is a natural response when trying new approaches.

The book is written in the order of the acronym **TEAM**: **T**hought + **E**motion + **A**ction = **M**anifestation. The next chapter on Thoughts addresses textual analysis since most acting performances start with a text or script. Each of the following chapters build upon the acting examples set up in previous chapters to help you understand the inter-relatedness of each of the TEAM parts. The book culminates with a final chapter that provides exercises to help you personally connect with the elements of the TEAM and put theory into practice. Although the book is written in a specific order, you are encouraged to approach the study of your role in whatever order satisfies the needs of the script; however, it is very important that you ultimately include all parts of the TEAM.

Stories from actual play rehearsals, auditions, acting classes, and acting workshops are included throughout the book to illustrate how the TEAM is used. *Try This* exercises are also provided to assist in connecting acting theories with daily activities and behaviors. The book concludes with side coaching instructions, and short plays to use for exercises and application of the TEAM.

The book is designed as a workbook, so you can hold the book while you try exercises, test open scenes, and refer to word lists during scene work. You are encouraged to write in this book, filling in answers on exercises, highlighting inspiring sections, and jotting notes in the margins. Mark pages with sticky notes so you can easily find the checklists, concepts, exercises or instructions that you want to revisit regularly. This book's objective is to become one of your favorite acting companions. So, read on and discover the power of the TEAM.

"Perhaps we are taught to avoid trouble [so] actors don't realize they must go looking for it. The more conflict actors find, the more interesting the performance."

– Michael Shurtleff

Chapter 2

Thoughts

Thought (noun): intention, purpose, expectation, imagination, consideration, opinion, belief, reasoning power, application of mental attention[7]

Thoughts is a general category that encompasses the character's thinking. Thoughts include the character's personal objectives, self reflections, sense of identity, reactions, beliefs, justifications, back-story, personal obstacles and desires. Thoughts are explored in this chapter by introducing methods for identifying the character's needs, objectives, goals, and victories. The use of Action Words and their relationships to these areas are also covered, along with steps for connecting these discoveries to the process of acting a role.

The first lesson in preparing a role using a Thought approach, or MVP, is to understand the character's objective. As you read on and learn more about how objectives affect acting, consider this: "If the bare essence of acting with someone in a scene is to know why your character stays in a room with another character, what keeps your character in the room? Why not leave?" The answer is in the objective.

Objectives

Objectives, often called intentions, motivate many of the character's actions. Objectives are the driving forces behind many aspects of human behavior. Would

7. "The Online Etymology Dictionary," accessed September 1, 2012, http://www.etymonline.com.

you get in a car and start the engine if you didn't know where you were going and for what reason? If you continued in the car down the road, with no objective in mind, you would find yourself aimlessly driving down random streets, floundering in your own indecision. Would you walk into a meeting that you scheduled with someone if you didn't have a goal for the discussion and outcome? How strange would it be if you started putting ingredients in a bowl without knowing what you intended to make? These examples may appear absurd, when started with no clear intention, yet stepping into an acting role requires the same clarity—an objective. Stanislavski referred to objectives as "buoys to mark the channel," guiding the actor through the proverbial creative waterways of the play's action. He recognized that many actors skip this process or are unable to analyze a script for playable actions, and so they "find themselves forced to handle a multitude of superficial, unrelated details, so many that they become confused and lose all sense of the larger whole."[8]

When I ask an actor, "What is your objective?" the beginning actor rarely has an answer, or she states an inactive objective that lacks passionate drive or dedication toward a specific outcome. An example of inactive objectives might be, "*to be left alone*" or "*to ask him a question*" or "*to joke with her.*" Laurence Olivier once said that the actor's job was to "lead the audience by the nose to the thought." An actor without a plan for action is simply lost, unprepared, and a passive victim of the circumstances. How interesting would that be to watch?

Searching For the Lost Puppy

I watch auditions for our upcoming production of Neil Labute's The Shape of Things, *searching for the right actor to play the part of Adam, an intelligent yet geeky lost soul of a college student, willing to do nearly anything to be loved. I tell the actors that I am looking for someone to capture the lost puppy quality in Adam that motivates this character to do anything and everything that his girlfriend, Evelyn, asks him to do. I tell them, "He wants more than anything to be loved and accepted by a beautiful woman, but he is awkward about all his attempts—like a puppy who has not yet grown into his paws."*

The actors auditioning struggle to play this complex character. Scene after scene I watch young actors portray depressed or angry men

8. Constantine Stanislavski, *An Actor Prepares* (New York: Routledge, 1989), 111-127.

who sulk around the stage, trapped in inactive choices, playing only the emotions of being lost, rather than pursuing the objective of being found and accepted. They weakly attempt the objectives I suggest or they remain focused on the emotions of being lost. Their performances come across stiff, withdrawn, and repetitively mundane as they mope around scenes without truly investing in the moment to moment actions and reactions of a character in pursuit of something positive—like love, affection, and acceptance. They seem unable to honestly react to what others in the scene do or say since their focus is so internally anchored in dwelling on their own emotions.

I sigh as I watch these proceedings, offering side coaching in hopes that one of these actors will have the skill to truly connect with this character's desires and objectives. I sit and worry, "Will I find an actor who can fully personify this character?"(This story is continued later in this chapter.)

Try This:

The next time you watch a good movie, go back and re-watch scenes that were particularly engaging. Focus your attention on the character that appears to be the driving force of action in that scene. Then ask yourself, "What does she want?" and "Is this scene interesting to me because she is sincerely dedicated to obtaining what she wants?" Most likely you will be pinpointing the actor's objective in that role. Can you figure out the objectives of the other characters in the scene and how their objectives are also making the scene so engaging?

Opposing Objectives Create Conflict

The key to drama is conflict or opposing actions. Without driven passionate actions, conflict is non-existent. The well regarded acting coach, Michael Shurtleff, once said of conflict, "An actor is looking for conflict. Conflict is what creates drama. Plays are not written about our everyday lives or the moments of peace and placidity, but about the extraordinary, the unusual, the climaxes."

Conflict will only rise out of a situation where people are truly dedicated to their own outcomes, pitched against others who have opposing desires. Clear, active objectives are absolutely necessary in creating fully dimensional and fervently driven characters. They result in dynamic performances reflecting the epitome of the human condition. Yet actors struggle constantly to pinpoint the strongest, conflict-centered, choice for an objective. Shurtleff offers an explanation: "Perhaps we are taught to avoid trouble [so] actors don't realize they must go looking for it. The more conflict actors find, the more interesting the performance."[9] In order to identify strong objectives, an actor must work like a detective, searching for the conflict and clues in the script to determine the modus operandi of the character. This investigative process will eventually provide strong active motives. Eventually, with practice this process will become habitual and instinctive. However, in the beginning, it may take some time to develop these skills and learn to avoid the common pitfalls of weak choices and inactive objectives.

Three Types of Objectives

There are three types of objectives: Scene, Main, and Super Objective. The difference between these objectives is the expanse of time over which the objective influences the character's actions. The Super Objective is what the character wants for her life.

[**Example**] In David Auburn's play *Proof*, Catherine is the daughter of a world-renowned mathematician who suffered from mental illness late in his life and has recently died. Catherine's Super Objective could be *to achieve recognition for my own superior talents in math.* (Notice that Objective Statements are always written in first person, to reflect the character's point of view). She grew up in the shadow of her father's success, struggling all her life to make her own mark.

This Super Objective would easily span the duration of much of Catherine's life. However, during the course of the play *Proof*, her sister Claire consistently suspects Catherine of exhibiting tendencies for the same mental illness their

9. Shurtleff, Michael, *Audition* (New York: Walker Publishing, 1978), 43.

father had; meanwhile, Catherine keeps seeing and speaking to her dead father who appears periodically in the play. Although Catherine still continues to be driven by her Super Objective, the opposing forces of her questionable sanity require immediate attention during the period of the play.

The Main Objective is the character's goal for the duration of the script. Throughout the play *Proof*, Catherine must resolve this question of her sanity and hopefully continue on the path of her personal quest. Therefore, Catherine's focus for the duration of the play, and her Main Objective, is t*o prove to everyone, including myself, that I am sane.* She still has the overall drive to be recognized as a mathematician, but her need for clarity concerning her sanity supersedes the Super Objective because the urgency to resolve this conflict is greater than the overall career goal.

The Scene Objective is a smaller unit of urgency and action determined by the given circumstances in a scene. The Scene Objective is still motivated by the needs of the Super Objective and Main Objective; however, when a character deals with the given circumstances of each scene, those immediate priorities must be solved first before continuing on the path to the Main Objective.

[**Example**] During the play *Proof*, Catherine becomes attracted to her father's graduate-level research assistant, Hal. He tells her that he has always been attracted to her, and after a night of lovemaking Catherine feels she can trust him with a secret, a groundbreaking mathematical proof she wrote. Her Scene Objective could be *to build a trusting relationship with Hal by sharing my secret.* However, Hal questions whether she wrote the proof, claiming that it could have been written by her father. Later on, Catherine tries to convince Hal and Claire that she did indeed write the proof herself, desperate to have one of them believe her.

In this scene, her Scene Objective could be *to make them believe me.* Both examples of Scene Objectives still serve as supporting actions for the Main Objective and Super Objective.

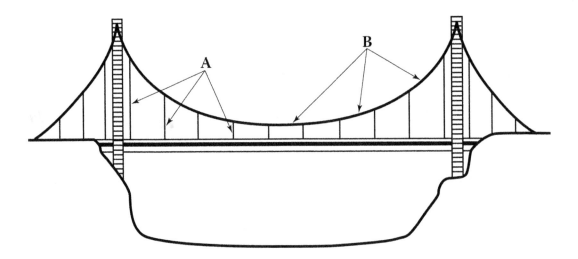

To better understand how the structure of Super, Main, and Scene Objectives support each other, consider the structural support of a suspension bridge. Like the many support beams *(A in the diagram above)* over which a suspension bridge is stretched, the Scene Objectives have their own immediate duty: to support their particular area of the bridge's structure. However, the Main Objective is like the long stretch of cable across the top of the bridge *(B in the diagram above)*, stretching across the great divide, bringing the character from one destination to the next, and yet supported by the individual structures that make up the entire bridge. The Main Objective in a script is often referred to as the Through-Line for the character. Much like that main cable stretching the distance of the bridge, the Main Objective drives the character's needs and desires through the entire script. The Super Objective is the overall journey the character wants to take. By reaching the other side of the bridge (the goal of the Main Objective), your character is that much closer to her Super Objective, which is still far off in the distance.

Try This:

Since these basic acting theories are rooted in true human behavior, take a moment to consider your own life. What would your Super Objective be? Now think back on a time when you worked hard to accomplish a goal that would take you further in this direction. It could be a time span of a few days or weeks. Can you identify this as your Main Objective at the time? Create a phrase with an Action Word and one subject—like *to acquire a well-paid job* or *to earn a degree*—for this Main Objective and see how it would support your Super Objective. Then, recall a short moment within the time frame of the Main Objective event where a different urgency arose that needed resolving before you could continue with the Main Objective. This would be your own real life Scene Objective. See if you can identify other Scene Objectives within the time frame of the Main Objective.

Selecting Strong Objectives

In order to select objectives with high stakes that are driven by a sense of urgency, the objective must be strongly rooted in basic human needs, like: love, recognition, and education. This also creates a universal quality to the objective, allowing any witness of the performance to immediately recognize and relate to this need, thereby strengthening audience empathy with the performance. We can all relate to the need to be loved, to want recognition for something we do well, or for the need to know more.

There are a number of human needs theories and models illustrating basic human needs and motivations. One well-regarded model is Maslow's Hierarchy of Needs, developed by Abraham Maslow and first published in 1954 with five basic needs. Later developments, made by Maslow and other psychologists and theorists, added more layers to the original five-layered hierarchy, eventually concluding with eight basic needs. Maslow's Hierarchy, later interpreted by placing the needs in a pyramid diagram, is displayed on the following page listing the qualities of the eight needs.[10]

---

10. Abraham H. Maslow, *Motivation and Personality*, Second Edition (New York: Harper and Row, 1970), 72-75.

The pyramid from top to bottom reads:

- Spiritual Needs
- Ultimate Fulfillment Needs
- Beauty Needs
- Cognitive Needs
- Ego Needs
- Social Needs
- Security Needs
- Body Needs

1. Body Needs - Feelings of sated hunger, thirst, sleep, sex, physical comfort, well-being, health, energy, and euphoria

2. Security Needs - Feelings of safety, security, protection, peace, lack of danger and threat

3. Social Needs - Feelings of belongingness, love and being love-worthy, acceptance, and affection—and identifying with a group, family, co-workers, friends

4. Ego Needs - Feelings of self-reliance, self respect, self-esteem, achievement, competence, independence, recognition, prestige, success

5. Cognitive Needs - Feelings of growth, self-realization, maturity, curiosity, learning, knowing, logic, philosophical and/or religious satisfaction; and feelings of unified connections and values

6. Beauty Needs - Feelings of valuing aesthetics, beauty, thrills, delight, comforts, pleasing the senses, perfection, symmetry, rightness, suitability

7. Ultimate Fulfillment Needs - Feelings of self-fulfillment, self-actualization, peak experiences, high values and taste, reaching one's ultimate potential

8. Spiritual Needs - Feelings of exaltation, mystic experiences, orgasmic emotion, ecstasy, spirituality, nirvana, helping others achieve self-actualization

Maslow's Hierarchy of Needs

The foundation of human behavior is need. Needs are both biological and psychological. The biological needs are the lowest three levels in the hierarchy: Body, Security, and Love/Affection. The higher levels are psychological: Ego, Knowledge, Beauty, Fulfillment, and Spiritual.[11] The majority of the needs are psychological, and according to this hierarchy, our thoughts and beliefs influence the majority of our actions. In addition, when experiencing biological needs, we respond to these needs by forming thoughts about how to satisfy them. For example, we have thoughts about how we should and should not satisfy our needs for love and affection, food consumption, and appropriate shelter. It is quite a common reaction to express thoughts of regret if a person feels as if he made a bad choice in the pursuit of love or food. Likewise we form beliefs about what is good food or an appropriate place to live. We can surmise then that the character's thoughts and beliefs can be a strong basis, and ultimately a Through-Line, for building the character's TEAM.

Body Needs form the base of the triangle, representing the most basic physiological needs for all human survival. According to Maslow's theory, the lower needs are deficiency motivators, which must be satisfied before one can gratify higher-level needs, or growth motivators. Once lower-level needs are satisfied, we can essentially aspire to higher interests and needs.[12] Below are some examples of how lower needs may highjack the higher needs:

1. A person who is starving must satisfy the Body need first before he can satisfy the higher Cognitive or Beauty needs, like furthering his education or creating art.

2. An individual who does not feel safe will satisfy her Security needs before she can address her Ultimate Fulfillment needs, like going on a book tour to celebrate her new book, or going up for a partner position at her law firm.

11. Abraham H. Maslow, *Towards a Psychology of Being*, Third Edition (New York: John Wiley & Sons, Inc., 1998), 21-43.
12. Maslow, *Motivation and Personality*, 72.

3. A businessman with the Main Objective, *to become a CEO with my company*, but who has a client who threatens his life just before he is going into a meeting with the company partners, will change his immediate need to Security, *to save my life*. His Security need temporarily supersedes his Ultimate Fulfillment need, to become a CEO.

The lower, more biological needs will most likely override the higher, social and self-fulfilling needs, even if a person was already in pursuit of satisfying the higher need. In most cases, the urgency of the immediate lower need rising up will demand attention and satisfaction before the higher needs can be addressed again.

In some cases, however, the character's basic physiological needs do not override the higher needs like self-fulfillment or transcendence, particularly if they are using a base need as a strong tactical choice to get them to a higher need. For example, in Ben Kingsley's portrayal of Gandhi in the movie *Gandhi*, he depicts the true story of a man who goes on a hunger strike as a strong tactical choice to stop hatred and war. Here we have an example of a conscious device used to override a basic human need in order to obtain a higher need, as well as attempt to bring others to higher levels by his example.

Needs Are Interpreted Individually

It is important to understand that these needs are individually interpreted by the person experiencing the need, and according to the given circumstances. When using Maslow's diagram, you must consider the given circumstances of varying cultures, socio-economic conditions, religious beliefs, and personal beliefs. Consider how many different ways people might perceive sex: as a biological need, a social need, or a community building need. Additionally, one person's need and her understanding of when that need is satisfied can be quite different from another person's interpretation.

[**Example**] Consider two people in pursuit of satisfying the Cognitive need for education. One person may feel that he has learned enough once he has satisfied society's requirement of a high school education. He may choose to move on to satisfy his Beauty needs with the nice car and pleasant living conditions. His Cognitive need is satisfied, and he moves to a Beauty need. However, another person may interpret her Cognitive need as being unsatisfied until she gains a college or graduate school degree. She will put more attention and action into satisfying that need, and delay gratification of the higher Beauty needs.

When working on character analysis, it is important to approach the script like a detective. Determine what your character's individual needs are, how these needs relate to the given circumstances, when each need has been satisfied, and what need the character moves to satisfy next. This may be challenging if your character's values contradict your own, or if these values are far removed from your own life experience. For example, some may assume that anyone who is homeless would not be able to pursue the higher-level needs. However, when we recognize that all these levels are individually interpreted by each person's own beliefs, values, cultural background and levels of personal tolerance, then there are many possibilities to consider for each character.

The Underground

I am acting in a new play, written and directed by one of my professors in graduate school. It is a story about homeless people living in the New York City underground tunnels, which connect subways, maintenance tunnels, and deserted pathways for old trains. I play a woman in the underground who is constantly organizing protests and public demonstrations concerning employee rights, taxes, and anything associated with government or big business control issues.

As a young actress still developing my craft, I struggle with my portrayal of this character. I keep dwelling on her homeless situation, preferring to focus on her poor living conditions, basing this choice on my own interpretation of her lack. My director pushes me to be more active, to find the joy in her speeches and the blissful excitement of her protests. However, in my own short-sightedness, I interpret her grandstanding as angry, rebellious, and sad. I am failing to see how the role could be played the way the director and playwright indicate.

One day, outside of rehearsal, I study and ponder the script with a good friend and director, Robert, who always seems to help me see what I am missing in my acting. He points out to me that this woman, who used to own a big health food store in the city, became frustrated with the bureaucracy of business and government and decided to give it all up and live "on the streets." He points out that this move to the streets was her decision—not something she perceived as a condition forced upon her. She likes not having to pay taxes, rent, or utility bills and not putting her energy into managing a business. She revels in the freedom found in the underground and now can focus her attention on social action, rallying other homeless individuals to change policies while she works on writing a healthy cookbook. These are all things she could not do when she was struggling to keep her business going and pay bills. This realization that she was not acting like a victim of her homeless situation and was indeed reveling in its freedom suddenly opened my mind to an entirely new understanding of my character's motivations.

*To support her Body needs of food, drink, and warmth, she manages to make an income by collecting cans and bottles off the street and turning them in for refunds at the local recycle center. She satisfies her Security and Social needs by creating her own supportive family of homeless individuals who develop a security protocol so that all in the underground feel a sense of order and safety. With her lower needs met to **her** satisfaction, she is able to focus on her Ultimate Fulfillment pursuits.*

Once I made this discovery, I was able to find all the joy, enthusiasm, and vitality in my need-based objective pursuits. My director was pleased with the results and I was liberated in my portrayal of this unique role.

If you base the character's objectives in clearly identified basic needs, interpreted and justified by the character's given circumstances, you will have a strong, active basis for your acting throughout the story. Although there are other human needs theories besides Maslow's Hierarchy, his model clearly demonstrates how humans may prioritize one need over the other. Basic human needs are universal, regardless of variations in theoretical models, and provide a reliable strategy for an actor to use in detecting and developing strong objectives.

Exercise
Personal Statement Exploration to Help Determine Needs

Consider a character you are playing, or could play in the future. Read the entire script, looking for any expressive words or behaviors that might provide you with clues to your character's perceptions of these eight needs. Is your character exhibiting behaviors that reveal comfort and satisfaction with some of the needs? Does your character make statements about being unfulfilled by one or two needs? Imagine yourself "in the shoes of your character," and then read the following statements and check the box next to the ones you feel could be true for your character.

☐ **A**   I feel self-reliant, competent, and independent. I am satisfied with the amount of recognition and respect I receive from others. I do feel proud of my accomplishments and abilities.

☐ **B**   I feel I belong to, and am loved by, a supportive, affectionate group or family. I have good relationships with co-workers and friends and feel accepted for who I am.

☐ **C**   I value and actively collect beautiful things that bring comfort and pleasure to my life. An environment in balanced harmony, which is pleasing to my senses, is important to me and provides a feeling that all is right in my world.

☐ **D**   It is important for me to pursue knowledge of things beyond what is necessary for my work. I am curious and enjoy investigating and discussing various topics and beliefs with people. By doing so, I feel I learn more about myself and am better able to connect and understand other people's values.

☐ **E**   I feel that my body is reasonably satisfied with regular meals, sleep, and comfortable living conditions. I have sufficient and reliable comforts when it comes to my home environment.

☐ **F**   I actively participate and relish in peak experiences. I feel this engagement helps me stretch and reach my ultimate potential. I do tend to set very high standards for myself, as well as for others, and pride myself on having good taste.

☐ **G** I generally feel safe and secure and do not feel as if I need to protect myself from threat or danger. I am rarely, if ever, exposed to uncontrolled circumstances where chaos or violent behaviors would threaten my sense of peace or productivity.

☐ **H** I regularly have feelings of emotional exaltation and ecstasy and often pursue mystic experiences. I define myself as spiritual. I enjoy helping others achieve this state of being, and will put great effort into encouraging others to join this self-actualized way of life.

The boxes checked represent the needs you feel are currently satisfied. The boxes left un-checked represent the needs you feel are currently unsatisfied. A person is most likely going to pursue satisfaction of any low-level needs before going after the higher-level needs.[13]

To interpret which statements match to the needs in the hierarchy, refer to the list of Maslow's Hierarchy below, beginning with the matching letter from the statements listed previously.

E   1. **Body Needs** - Feelings of sated hunger, thirst, sleep, sex, physical comfort, well-being, health, energy, and euphoria

G   2. **Security Needs** - Feelings of safety, security, protection, peace, lack of danger and threat

B   3. **Social Needs** - Feelings of belongingness, love and being love-worthy, acceptance, and affection—and identifying with a group, family, co-workers, friends

A   4. **Ego Needs** - Feelings of self-reliance, self respect, self-esteem, achievement, competence, independence, recognition, prestige, success

D   5. **Cognitive Needs** - Feelings of growth, self-realization, maturity, curiosity, learning, knowing, logic, philosophical and/or religious satisfaction; and feelings of unified connections and values

C   6. **Beauty Needs** - Feelings of valuing aesthetics, beauty, thrills, delight,

13. Ibid.

comforts, pleasing the senses, perfection, symmetry, rightness, suitability

F   7. **Ultimate Fulfillment Needs** - Feelings of self-fulfillment, self-actualization, peak experiences, high values and taste, reaching one's ultimate potential

H   8. **Spiritual Needs** - Feelings of exaltation, mystic experiences, orgasmic emotion, ecstasy, spirituality, nirvana, helping others achieve self-actualization

---

Try This:

Considering your own life, complete the exercise: Personal Statement Exploration to Help Determine Needs. Use your personal life as a basis for checking the statements you feel are true. Consider these questions as you complete the exercise, possibly doing the exercise many times as you contemplate each question. What needs are you addressing with your actions? What need are you pursuing by reading this text? What need are you generally satisfying this week or during a few days of this week? What need do you feel you are trying to satisfy with your long-range goals? As you answer these questions, you are identifying your own need-base for a personal Scene Objective, Main Objective, and Super Objective. Practice this self-observation occasionally as you are in the midst of an action. Ask yourself, "What basic human need am I working to satisfy right now?" The more you practice this observation, the more easily it will come to you when you are investigating a character's needs in an acting role.

Victories Motivate Objectives

As we approach an important moment in our lives, we often visualize the desired outcome. When we attain that intended outcome, we are victorious, or celebrating the success of our achievement. Visualizing this desired outcome, before and throughout the event, is using a victory to motivate an objective.

[Example] The business man, referred to previously, who aspires to become CEO may visualize the company partners inviting him into their grand office, so they can stand, shake his hand and say, "Welcome to the top!" This type of inner monologue can be running in his mind before the event occurs. It can also run like a recording in his mind during the important moment, as real-time commentary of the current event. This expected outcome will then influence his thoughts and feelings throughout the scene. If he is met with an unexpected situation, he will react as if this was not truly what he wanted. What if the partners did not stand upon his entrance, but instead were very busy talking about something serious? He would walk in, hoping they would greet him, but receiving no greeting, and actually no attention at all, he would then react to this change in expectations. He would also apply various tactics throughout the scene that he hopes will help him get the focus back to his objective, so that he can achieve that desired victory.

By keeping our thoughts focused on this very detailed and highly desired victory, our behavior reflects honest reactions when receiving the unexpected, and our actions are motivated toward a very specific outcome. When we are invested in a highly desirous victory, we will try many different tactics to achieve the victory, by keeping our eye-on-the-prize.

When an actor is having a difficult time determining what her Scene Objective is, I will simply ask the actor, "What specific thing could the other character in the scene with you do or say that would be the ultimate win for your character?" The answer to this question would be an example of a victory. Often the actor can state this example of a victory far more easily than she can state her Objective Statement because it is a clear vision of a desired outcome. From this point, the actor can create an Objective Statement. The victory is a more specific outcome for the objective. The victory must be in line with the needs and desires of the objective; it simply provides a specific cap or ending point for the objective.

Imagine a time when you are going to see someone you have not seen in a long time. You might visualize in your mind how that person would look and act, what they would say when they see you, what you two would do together, as well as what you hope to gain by such a visit. As you meet up with your friend, these visualizations will greatly affect how you behave as you interact in the situation. Such visualizations and their influences on our actions are common in human behavior.

[Example] A Scene about Visiting an Old Friend

Consider these simple events, or scenes around the premise of Visiting An Old Friend. Here are three possible activities a person might engage in while visiting with an old friend.

(1)   Get a tour of my friend's new house
(2)   Indulge in a fancy dinner at our favorite restaurant
(3)   Play a game of basketball together

How would you conduct yourself if you had the following victories, or specific desired outcomes, attached to these scenarios?

(1a) Get a tour of my friend's new house
  (Victory) "He will say he always loved me."
(2a) Indulge in a fancy dinner at our favorite restaurant
  (Victory) "She will remember my birthday and treat me to dinner"
(3a) Play a game of basketball together
  (Victory) "I will finally beat him in the game."

Can you see how this visualized victory could affect your actions? Now, imagine completely different victories for all three situations.

(1b) Get a tour of my friend's new house
  (Victory) "He will help me buy a house in his exclusive
  neighborhood."
(2b) Indulge in a fancy dinner at our favorite restaurant
  (Victory) "She will apologize for our fight, putting it all behind us."
(3b) Play a game of basketball together
  (Victory) "He will give me news of my ex-girlfriend."

Even if all the circumstances in scenes 1a and 1b were the same—same dialogue, same blocking—the actions and outcomes would none the less be dramatically different. All of this is due to your needs, objectives, and perceived victory. Pursuing an objective without knowing when the action should end leaves you with no vision, no horizon to focus on, and no perceived ending point for your character's actions. It is important to conceive of a clear victory for the character's objective. Ideally, the Objective Statement will allude to this victory.

[Example] Here are Objective Statements for the possible scenes and victories mentioned above in Visiting An Old Friend:

(1a) Get a tour of my friend's new house
(Objective in Social Need) To charm him back into my life
(Victory) "He will say he always loved me."

(2a) Indulge in a fancy dinner at our favorite restaurant
(Objective in Social Need) To celebrate my birthday with an old friend
(Victory) "She will remember my birthday and treat me to dinner."

(3a) Play a game of basketball together
(Objective in Ego Need) To distinguish myself as the better athlete
(Victory) "He will lose the game."

___

(1b) Get a tour of my friend's new house
(Objective in Ego Need) To acquire real estate advice from my successful friend
(Victory) "He will agree to help me buy a house in his exclusive neighborhood."

(2b) Indulge in a fancy dinner at our favorite restaurant
(Objective in Social Need) To repair my friendship
(Victory) "She will apologize for our fight, putting it all behind us."

(3b) Play a game of basketball together
(Objective in Social Need) To soothe my broken heart with a

game of basketball

(Victory) "He will give me news of my ex-girlfriend."

We have taken several common events and created distinctly different scenes. Actors playing out each scene would exhibit entirely new behaviors due to the changes in objectives and desired victories.

The selection of the victory is as important as finding clear active wording for the Objective Statement. Let's look at how the different victories affect scene (1a) Get a tour of my friend's new house, with the Objective in Social Need.

[Example 1] New Victory: *He will ask me out for dinner tonight.* This victory, although still based in a Social Need, has less urgency than does a confession of love. It is a bit more casual, yet still focused on a desired outcome for building a relationship. Your behavior in this scene would be different than if you were searching for love.

[Example 2] New Victory: *We will have passionate sex together this afternoon.* This character will behave quite differently during this scene with the desired outcome placed in physical sex, rather than an outcome of stating one's love.

Notice that the basic human need motivating the actions in these victories has shifted from example to example. *To have sex* is more of a Body need, and *To get him to say he loves me* is more of a Social need. If you are driven by a Body need, your actions will be much more physical, using flirtatious looks and gestures that include physical touch, which all support signals for sensuality and sex. If you are motivated by the Social need of love, a deeper and higher-level need, your interactions are motivated more from the head with sentimental, romantic, or thoughtful behaviors, and they would be less physical. Selecting a specific victory for your objective directly affects the types of Action Tactics and Emotion Tactics (covered in later chapters) you will attempt throughout the scene.

Raising the Stakes

It is important to select a victory that is extremely difficult to achieve. By doing so you *raise the stakes* of the scene, or infuse the scene with urgency and conflict. A game or a challenge is always much more interesting to watch if we know the odds against winning are very high. When a character achieves a victory, it is a major accomplishment in the life of the character. So much so, that the victory is rarely accomplished. The character's constant, urgent motivation for this victory is what drives her actions in a scene. If a character accomplishes her victory, the given scene is over, and the scene ends with her reveling in that victory.

When selecting a victory for your scene, make sure it is so difficult to achieve that it may never actually happen. As you look at the scene, ask yourself if your character appears to have won something big by the end of the scene. If so, she has achieved her victory and you need to simply determine what that was. However, in most cases, your character is still struggling at the end of the scene, with the action being cut off by a shift to a new scene. In most cases the victory is not easily offered up by the script, so determining your victory will take a bit more imagination and detective work.

Remember that the core of dramatic action is conflict. If the victory is achieved, the conflict is over. The structure of most scripts delays the winning of victories until the very end of the story, and then only certain characters will achieve such victories. It is important to recognize this element of dramatic structure when selecting objectives and victories. Be aware of when your character is still searching and working toward a win, and when he's celebrating when a victory has been won. The audience is well aware of this struggle-and-win pattern. Consider any play or movie where you watched a character that you considered to be an underdog. As the story progressed and you empathized with his struggle to overcome great obstacles, you could probably tell exactly what his objective was and perhaps even guess at his desired victory. If the actor playing the underdog was doing his acting well, you could tell exactly when he finally achieved that victorious moment. He would express a cathartic moment or meaningful recognition for this great achievement, and so would you, as an audience member taking the journey with him.

What You Want—NOT What You Don't Want

Objectives and Victories should be stated in terms of what you, the character, want to achieve, not focused on what you don't want. Too often an actor will make a choice that focuses all her attention on what she does not want to happen, not realizing that this keeps her from truly understanding and going after what her character does want. This actor is often focusing more on the obstacles, rather than the objectives and victories. Placing the character's attention here could bog down the action with only the negative aspects of the character's journey, leaving the actor and the audience in a place where they are unable to identify what actually motivates the character.

[**Examples**] Objectives and victories based in what a character does not want would be like these: *to get her to stop talking about her ex-boyfriend, to avoid another fight with my father about my clothes,* and *to get him to stay out of my room.*

These examples do not display an apparent passion or drive toward a greater need or desire. Can you identify a clear human need in these examples? Most likely not, since they are not clearly anchored in a strong need. If you take each of these examples and focus instead on a basic human need, they might look like the examples below.

[**Examples**] Focusing on what a character wants, these objectives could be redirected like this: *to prove to her that I am the only true love of her life (Social need), to convince my father that my clothes are common fashions of today (Beauty need),* and *to get him to respect my privacy (Security need).*

Making passionate, need-based choices that provide a strong through-line of action will provide your acting work with greater depth and urgency.

Victory Statement Checklist

☐ Is the victory placed in the actions of your scene partner?

☐ Is the victory stated in the second person: "He will…" or "She will…"?

☐ Is the victory stated in positive terms of what will be done, not what won't be done?

☐ Is the statement kept to one simple sentence with one action verb and one subject?

☐ Is the victory in line with the intentions of the Scene Objective?

☐ Is the victory challenging to achieve, but conceivable?

☐ If the victory is accomplished, is it achieved by the very end of the scene?

Doorway Visualizations to Victories

A Doorway Visualization is imagining what could be going through your character's mind just before entering a scene, and then using those thoughts to affect your character's actions and reactions. Creating a Doorway Visualization can help you identify a scene victory. Applying the Doorway Visualization as a pre-scene preparation is also an excellent approach for making your actions and reactions look and feel fresh, unplanned, and focused on reacting off others in a scene.

Let's imagine a scene in a play or movie where a character is entering a room with a very important objective to accomplish.

[Examples]
- *To convince the board that I can lead them well*
- *To empower my team to win the championship*
- *To tell her I want to marry her*
- *To confess I stole money from them*

Then, picture this character standing outside of a room, facing the doorway to the room just before the scene begins. What would your character visualize for the upcoming scene's outcome? Write a Doorway Visualization for a scene, using the guidelines provided below. After you complete the visualization, see if you can determine the Victory Statement for the scene. It is very important to note that the most effective Doorway Visualization does not match what actually happens in the scene, but is what the character wishes or believes will happen. Use your imagination well here and immerse yourself in the secret desires and/ or fears of your character. A Doorway Visualization does not always have to be a desire but can be motivated by the character's fears, guilt, or low self-esteem. For example, a character who is guilty of doing something wrong may have a Doorway Visualization that she has been caught, and she is walking into a confrontation, so her visualization includes the negative aspect of the accusation; however, she will also visualize strategies she would use to make the punishment less severe, or lie and accuse someone else, or make a bargain, etc. The visualization is the expectation of unfolding events, and how the character plans to navigate the unknown event in the near future.

Writing a Doorway Visualization

Compose a paragraph that expresses the inner monologue of your character's thoughts by beginning with **"While standing outside the room, I visualize the following outcome..."** and completing the visualization description using the following categories:

- How I will appear to those witnessing my actions
- What they will think of me
- What I will do
- What they will do in return
- What I will say
- What they will say in return
- What I will get in the end

Doorway Visualization Example

Objective: to convince the board that I can lead them well

While standing outside the room, I visualize the following outcome:
When I enter the room they will be impressed by the impeccable outfit I planned to wear, which screams, "Leader!" with its power colors and strong masculine lines. They will be a little skeptical of my ability to lead them, and I will need to convince them that I can. They will think I am too young and too inexperienced for the job. So, I will astound them with my expert advice, extremely well-organized presentation, and factual support of all examples presented. They will gradually let go of all doubts in my ability to lead them and lean forward, eager to hear my plans for our future. They will express their surprise and delight in my great ideas. I will end the presentation by asking them, "Are you with me 100% in the plans?" and they will unanimously agree and shake my hand. I will end the meeting knowing that I have their full support.

Victory Statement: They will honestly say they back my ideas 100%

Try This:

Watch the opening scenes of the movie, *A Few Good Men*. The first scene begins as the opening credits are completing, and the camera focuses on Lieutenant Commander Galloway (played by Demi Moore) as she prepares for a meeting. Listen as she practices for the meeting and essentially is working through her visualization, voicing her preferred dialogue with senior officers she is about to meet. Then watch as she enters the meeting and reacts to her given circumstances. Can you tell when she is met with obstacles, or actions that conflict with her visualization? Can you also see how she applies various tactics, in hopes of keeping the men focused on her desired outcome?

Applying Doorway Visualizations

Once you have written your Doorway Visualization for a scene, use these steps to apply this technique to your acting.

1. Immediately before a rehearsal or run-through of a scene, take a moment and read your visualization.

2. Then close your eyes and imagine it happening in the scene you are about to run.

3. Once you believe you are committed to that vision and the specific victory you desire, start the scene.

4. Pursue that victory with all your actions and emotions while also being true to the nature of your character and the scripted lines.

5. React openly and honestly when you don't get what you expect. Don't be afraid to be too big here. This is a rehearsal, where you are exercising the use of the Visualization to see what behavior will emerge when you commit to it. You can always pull back, or diminish the larger expressions of actions and reactions later on to acquire the right level for the final performance.

6. After the scene is over, review discoveries you made by applying the Doorway Visualization and make note of aspects you would like to keep, discard, or explore further.

Searching For the Lost Puppy Story (Part II)

As a director of the play, The Shape of Things, I am frustrated by the actors auditioning who keep dwelling on what the character doesn't want. Adam wants to find someone who will love him, but these actors keep making choices that isolate him from other characters in the scenes. Adam wants to be liked, but their delivery of Adam's joke lines are filled with sarcasm and anger. They are focusing on the negatives, and not the true wants and desires of Adam.

Finally, a handsome, slightly overweight forty-year-old man gets up to read. He interprets Adam with a shy smile and with eyes and shoulders slightly downcast, yet he exhibits a soft and eager "I want to be liked" quality. He gently fumbles through actions in scenes, listening intently to the actress with whom he reads, always exuding a low level of flirtatiousness, followed by a nervous giggle whenever he receives a compliment. This actor knew how to portray a man who truly wanted to be liked, who wanted to please others, but who also had personal obstacles of physical and social awkwardness that he was attempting to overcome through humor and intellect. This actor had all the parts of the TEAM aligned after following my suggestion: "He wants more than anything to be loved and accepted by a beautiful woman, but he is awkward about all his attempts—like a puppy who has not yet grown into his paws." This actor allowed Adam's thoughts, emotions, and actions to be modified from moment to moment due to the ever changing and shifting events around him. All behavior seemed based in the pursuit of satisfying this social need of love and affection. I had my Adam! This actor could fully embody all the necessary levels of this character's wants and needs. I knew an audience would empathize with his struggle and appreciate his sweet desperation to be loved. This actor could—and did—do that.

Applying Basic Needs to Objective Development

Below are Catherine's Objectives from the play *Proof* and how they look on Maslow's hierarchical triangle.

(1) **Super Objective**—*to achieve recognition for my own superior talents in math*, is an Ultimate Fulfillment need (#7 level).

(2) **Main Objective**—to prove to everyone, including myself, that I am sane, can be identified as an Ego need (#4 level) .

(3) **Scene Objectives**—to build a trusting relationship with Hal, and to make them believe me, are Social needs (#3 level), pursuing relationship and acceptance needs.

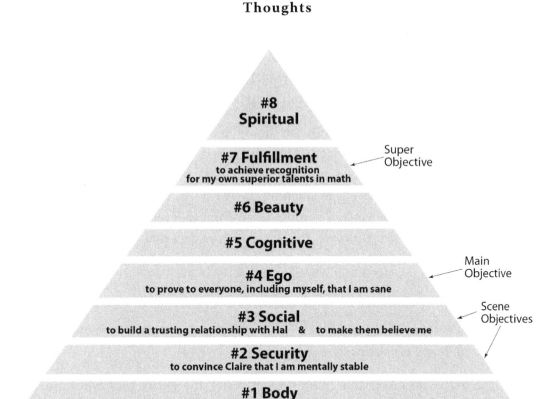

In this example of objectives placed on Maslow's triangle, Catherine's objectives stretch upwards, in a numerically ascending order: Scene Objectives (#3 Level), Main Objective (#4 Level), and Super Objective (#7 Level).

Occasionally, as discussed earlier, when lower-level needs rise up and must be satisfied—a Scene Objective will come along that is based in a lower-level need. For example, there are many times throughout the play that Catherine fears others may think she truly is insane, and so her need in a scene shifts temporarily to that of a Security need (#2 Level), like in this objective, "to convince Claire that I am mentally stable." Fearing she may be institutionalized, she works to regain her security, and then once gained, she returns to her previous place on the hierarchy as she works again toward that ultimate goal of achieving recognition.

The Super Objective is based in a need that is higher in the hierarchy than the Main Objective and Scene Objectives. As discussed before, the lower basic needs (Levels #1, #2, #3) manifest a greater urgency for satisfaction. A person who is starving, or feels unsafe, or who has lost the support of a loved one will not be concerned with beauty or knowledge until the lower-level need has been satisfied, or at least stabilized. When low-level needs emerge in scenes, they will temporarily supersede the Super Objective and Main Objective. Knowing this hierarchy can help the actor ascertain basic needs, why these needs vary from scene to scene, and why a character temporarily strays from the goals of the Main Objective.

If an actor chooses to identify the Main Objective as a lower-level need, the urgency to accomplish this objective may be raised, creating greater intensity in actions and reactions. Many action or thrill-based movies have characters who need to fulfill their safety needs throughout the story. The results are highly intense stories, where you rarely catch a glimpse of any higher-level needs like the Social, Ego, or Cognitive needs. However, the actor must realize that with this choice the Scene Objectives will be limited to the lower-level needs.

> **[Example]** Consider an actor selecting a Security need (Level #2) as the basis for Catherine's Main Objective, *to prove to everyone, including myself, that I am mentally stable.*

The actor who uses this Main Objective for the entire play will limit her needs for Scene Objectives to the lower-level hierarchy needs, #2 and below. She may have a brief moment in a scene where upper level needs are introduced and temporarily pursued; however, her Main Objective need will keep her focus down to a security level.

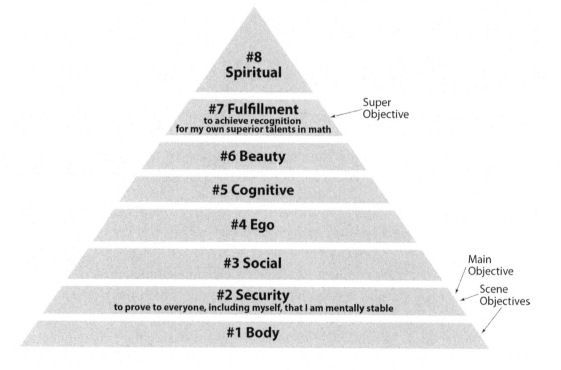

If this same actor places Catherine's Super Objective up in level #7, *to achieve recognition for my own superior talents in math*, even looking at the diagram, a victory for her Super Objective appears unreachable and unattainable. The Super Objective, although far into the future of the character's life, should have a sense of being achievable and conceivable to the character.

Conditions vs. Objectives

Some people might confuse the character's conditions—like an emotional state, physical limitation, and given environmental circumstances for objectives. For example, in *Proof* Catherine's sister Claire throws a party at the house after their father's funeral. Hal, a graduate student who studied with their father, comes out onto the porch to talk with Catherine. Far too often I have heard someone identify Catherine's objective for this scene as, *to get Hal to leave so I can properly mourn my father's death.* With this choice the actor can get trapped into playing only Catherine's condition, mourning the loss of her father. This is not an action that is actively in pursuit of an outcome from another person in the room. Additionally, the dialogue in the scene does not support the first part of the objective, *to get Hal to leave.* During this scene they talk about her father, her dress, and famous mathematicians. As the scene progresses, it becomes clear that Catherine knows a great deal more than Hal was initially aware of, and it appears that throughout the scene, Catherine might be pursuing the objective, *to determine what Hal's intentions are with me* or *to determine if Hal is capable of believing that I am indeed a brilliant mathematician.* Either of these objectives would be far more active than to simply want Hal to leave so she can mourn. It is perfectly acceptable for Catherine to feel emotions of sadness, depression, and fear as valid conditions coloring her behavior. However, the primary focus of a character's objective should not be to immerse in an emotional state, or play a condition.

The Depressed Catherine

I am watching a production of Proof, *produced by a professional theatre company. I have been excited all week about bringing my students to this performance because they have been reading and conducting in-depth scene studies of the needs and objectives of the play's characters.*

As the play unravels I watch the actor playing Catherine mope around the stage, depressed, angry, forlorn, and occasionally striking out at those around her. It becomes clear to me that she is basing her needs consistently in Security, and her preferred tactics are those of emotional withdrawal and self-pity. Her performance quickly becomes mundane and inactive, and I lose empathy for her character, who has clearly given up on herself as well.

However, her sister Claire is riveting. Claire has not given up on Catherine. She has clearly based her Main Objective in the much higher Cognitive (#5) need to learn as much about her sister as possible. It is so clear to the audience that Claire truly wants to understand what is troubling Catherine and how she can help her, that Claire wins our empathy, our admiration, and our hearts. By the end of the play we would do anything for Claire, but Catherine—we had given up on just as she had given up on herself.

My students learned some valuable acting lessons that day. The lessons from class about applying passion and conviction to strong objectives proved to be vital needs missing in one actor's performance, while my students witnessed the contrasting vibrancy of another actor who attended to these needs. The supportive evidence was right before their very eyes.

Needs and the Main Objective

The Main Objective is an overall strategy that a character uses throughout the life of the play or movie to fulfill an unsatisfied need. The primary need of the character will vary depending on who the character is and what the character's given circumstances are in the story. One character in a story may be working hard on a Security need while another is fulfilling a Cognitive need. Each person's needs vary greatly depending on their beliefs about their given circumstances. The basis of these beliefs and needs is the main source of dramatic conflict. By building your Main Objective on a specific and vital basic need, you will guarantee that your Scene Objectives and supportive behaviors have the potential for action, passion, and urgency.

Look at any play or movie genre and you will find common basic needs themes:

Romance — Social—people searching for loving relationships and acceptance

Thrillers — Security—desperate characters "running for their lives"

War Movies — Security—heroes protecting homeland and country

Mystery/Detective — Cognitive—clever people using elusive clues to solve mysteries

Competitive Sports — Fulfillment—professional athletes competing to be the best

Inspirational Stories — Fulfillment or Spirituality—highly regarded characters revealing life-affirming stories that lift us up

Identifying the needs of a character is actually quite simple when you narrow the list down to the basic eight areas of all human needs. Determining your character's Main Objective will become considerably easier when basing Objective Statements in these human needs.

To identify the Main Objective for your character:

(1) While reading the play, look for common themes in the scene objectives, and consider how they might point toward an overall goal for the duration of the play.

(2) Make note of any specific goals and desires that your character states. Consider what other characters say about your character's needs as well.

(3) Ask yourself, "Is there something specific that someone important to my character would do or say that would provide a clear victory for my character?"

(4) Compose a Main Objective Statement using the Main Objective Checklist.

Main Objective Checklist

☐ Is it anchored in a basic human need?

☐ Does it focus on one single outcome?

☐ Does it utilize only one Action Word?

☐ Does it motivate your actions throughout the play/movie?

☐ Is it supported by the events in your character's scenes?

☐ Is it stated in positive terms, focusing on what you want, not what you don't want?

☐ Is it a short, single-subject phrase, stated in the first person?

☐ Is the achievement of the outcome difficult, taking the entire action of the play/movie to accomplish, if accomplished at all?

☐ Is there a specific victory that would end all actions toward this outcome?

Talking About the Character Using "I"

As soon as you can, talk about your character using first person. For example, say things like, "I think I am searching for...," "I want this from him," or "I am not sure why I act like this in the scene." By talking about your character in the first person, you are already beginning the embodiment process by using wording that projects the belief that you are the character. If an actor talks about her character using "she" rather than "I," the actor will distance herself from the life of the character. The actor will end up commenting on the life of the character through her actions and behavior, rather than being in the moment and living through the character's experiences. You will notice that all objective and victory statements are worded in first person to support this embodiment transformation process.

Exercise
Basic Needs Motivating Objectives

Below are examples of Main and Scene Objectives for characters in plays and movies. Identify the need in Maslow's Hierarchy of Needs on which the objective is based.

1. To make him love me
   social Need

2. To protect her from herself
   security Need

3. To prove that this painting is a valued piece of art
   Beauty Need

4. To verify that God is my baby's father
   _ultimate fulfillm_Need

5. To win the race with honor.
   ultimate Need
   fulfilment

6. To do whatever it takes to get him to feed me
   Body Need

7. To protect my young witness from the murderers
   _security_Need

8. To discover groundbreaking research left by my mentor
   cognitive Need

9. To teach her that all things in life are based in numbers
   spiritual Need

10. To create a provocative and daring thesis project
    Cognitive Need

11. To empower my troops to make history by winning the battle
    ego Need

12. To make a baby with my best friend's willing husband
    ultimate Need
    fulilment?

13. To convince them that I am refreshing company
    _Actual___Need

14. To regain control over my home and sanctuary
    _security___Need

15. To secure my new position by befriending a senior faculty member
    _ego____Need

Maslow's Hierarchy of Needs[14]

1. **Body Needs** - Feelings of sated hunger, thirst, sleep, sex, physical comfort, well-being, health, energy, and euphoria

2. **Security Needs** - Feelings of safety, security, protection, peace, lack of danger and threat

3. **Social Needs** - Feelings of belongingness, love and being love-worthy, acceptance, and affection —and identifying with a group, family, co-workers, friends

4. **Ego Needs** - Feelings of self-reliance, self respect, self-esteem, achievement, competence, independence, recognition, prestige, success

5. **Cognitive Needs** - Feelings of growth, self-realization, maturity, curiosity, learning, knowing, logic, philosophical and/or religious satisfaction; and feelings of unified connections and values

6. **Beauty Needs** - Feelings of valuing aesthetics, beauty, thrills, delight, comforts, pleasing the senses, perfection, symmetry, rightness, suitability

7. **Ultimate Fulfillment Needs** - Feelings of self-fulfillment, self-actualization, peak experiences, high values and taste, reaching one's ultimate potential

8. **Spiritual Needs** - Feelings of exaltation, mystic experiences, orgasmic emotion, ecstasy, spirituality, nirvana, helping others achieve self-actualization

14. Maslow, *Motivation and Personality*, 72-75.

Thoughts

While you were filling in the needs for the objectives previously, you might have struggled as you considered a couple options for needs in some of the Objective Statements. This is a natural response when attempting to identify a need based only in an action statement. We are missing vital information surrounding the focus of the action—the given circumstances. Below is a list of the character's name and the title of the story associated with each of the objectives listed previously, followed by a brief description of the character's given circumstances. With this information, try identifying the needs for each Objective Statement again. Is it easier to do this task when you know more about the character's situation and beliefs?

1. **To make him love me**
   Social Need

   Julie in *Miss Julie.* Julie is a wealthy young lady who is attempting to win the affection of the butler, Jean.

2. **To protect her from herself**
   Cognitive Need

   Claire in *Proof.* Claire is concerned that her sister, Catherine, is mentally disabled like their father was.

3. **To prove that this painting is a valued piece of art**
   ego Need

   Serge in *Art.* Serge purchased a very expensive painting and is trying to convince his friends that it was worth the money he spent on it because it is art.

4. **To verify that God is my baby's father**
   spiritual Need

   Agnes in *Agnes of God.* Agnes is a young girl in a nunnery who recently and mysteriously gave birth to a baby. She is being questioned by a psychologist throughout the play about her situation.

5. **To win the race with honor.**
   Ultimate bla Need

   Harold Abraham in *Chariots of Fire.* Harold is an Olympic runner who desperately wants to win in the Olympics and honor his Jewish heritage.

6. **To do whatever it takes to get him to feed me**

_____*body*_____ Need

Kate in *Taming of the Shrew*. Kate has been married off to Petruchio who is determined to tame the shrew in her. After their long journey to her new home with him, he denies her food as he attempts to get her to speak sweetly to him.

7. **To protect my young witness from the murderers**

*cognitive*_____ Need

John Book in *Witness*. John is a NYC detective who is protecting a young Amish boy who witnessed a murder. They are hiding in Amish country with the boy and his family while he heals from a serious gunshot wound.

8. **To discover groundbreaking research left by my mentor**

_____*UF*_____ Need

Hal in *Proof*. Hal's mentor recently died and left an office filled with paperwork on his recent mathematical research. Hal offers to go through the paperwork to see if there is anything important left behind by his mentor.

9. **To teach her that all things in life are based in numbers**

spiritual Need

Robert in *Proof*. Robert is the father of Catherine, a young woman who could be the next mathematical genius but is not motivated to pursue her true talents.

10. **To create a provocative and daring thesis project**

_____*beauty*_____ Need

Evelyn in *The Shape of Things*. Evelyn is a graduate student in Art who has an edgy and daring idea for a thesis project, which requires a naïve human subject.

11. **To empower my troops to make history by winning the battle**

_____*UF*_____ Need

King Henry in *Henry V*. King Henry is delivering an inspiring speech about how these men will be honored for generations to come for their bravery and valor on this day, Saint Crispin's Day.

12. To make a baby with my best friend's willing husband
social   Need

Meg Jones in *The Big Chill*. Meg is a single woman who wants to be a mother. She asks her friend if she would be willing to let her husband sleep with her once, just so she can have a baby.

13. To convince them that I am refreshing company
social   Need

Blanche in *A Streetcar Named Desire*. Blanche, an overly affected and delicate southern lady, is seeking refuge at her sister's rustic and cramped living quarters in New Orleans. She attempts to win the support and affection of her sister's husband and his friends by showing that she brings class and style to their dismal existence.

14. To regain control over my home and sanctuary
security   Need

Shrek in *Shrek*. Shrek is an ogre who wants to regain his isolated living conditions, but he is inundated with unwelcome visitors disrupting his peace.

15. To secure my new position by befriending a senior faculty member
ego   Need

Nick in *Who's Afraid of Virginia Woolf?* Nick is a new faculty member at a private college. He and his wife are visiting the house of a senior faculty member whose wife happens to be the eccentric daughter of the college president.

These Objective Statement examples list situations for characters in plays and movies that range from a revered dramatic story like Shakespeare's *Henry V* to a simple children's animated movie like *Shrek*. One can see that identifying basic needs in a plot is a common and achievable process for any story, play, or film. No matter what the genre or how complicated or simple the plot is, by learning to identify these basic human needs, the actor has found a clear and reliable process for building the TEAM.

Try This:

Consider some characters in your own favorite plays and movies. See if you can determine the character's main need, according to Maslow's Hierarchy, and assign a Main Objective to the need. Then look at individual scenes and identify the needs of your character in each one. Try wording a Scene Objective based on the need in each scene.

Objectives vs. Action Tactics

Be careful not to mistake minor Action Tactics for Scene Objectives. An *Action Tactic* is the small action a character takes in order to achieve his Scene Objective. In a given scene, a character will attempt many different tactics in order to achieve his Scene Objective. Much like in life, when you are working hard to accomplish a difficult task, you will try many different approaches to accomplish this task and to overcome any obstacles that get in your way. For example, look at this very simple scene that could happen in your own life.

One evening while you are trying to study for a very important test, your good friend visits you. Throughout the following scene you:

- *Mention you need to study for an important test tomorrow*
- *Suggest a few other exciting things she can do this evening*
- *Invite her to go out to dinner tomorrow night*
- *Confess that you are tired this evening*
- *Ignore her stories at times and stare intently down at your books*
- *Question her reasons for visiting enough so that she finally admits she came to talk about how she wants to date a friend of yours*
- *Ask her to go pick up some take-out for dinner*
- *Call the friend that she is interested in and put her on the phone*
- *Ask if she would be willing to help you study*

Looking at the scene mentioned previously, what would you identify as your Scene Objective? Often an actor might say her character's objective is *to get my friend to leave, to get my friend a date*; or *to ignore my friend*, or *to be left alone.* Yes, these are all actions that the character attempts, but are they describing an overall and strong personal objective for the scene? To answer this, first ask yourself, "Is the overall action rooted in a basic human need for your character?" *To be left alone* or *to ignore* is certainly not one of the needs on the hierarchy. *To get your friend a date* may provide your friend with a Social need, but it does not serve *your* character's needs—so it would not be *your* objective. The second clue that these are not Scene Objectives is that they do not motivate all the actions in the scene from beginning to end. If you said your objective was *to be left alone*, you still have not pinpointed the proper Scene Objective because, at one point in the scene, you ask her to help you study. If your character truly wants to be left alone, then all actions would need to support this objective.

Some might then try to include all the actions they see in the Objective Statement; *to study for my test*, or *to get my friend to leave me alone; to visit with my friend but also study for my test*, and *to get my friend a date while I study for my test.* All of these examples are trying to accomplish more than one thing, which will divide your focus and keep you from fully committing to one objective for the scene. These examples are combining objectives with Action Tactics.

The key to a strong Objective Statement is to keep it to one singular action, which would include one Action Word and one subject, both in one short, direct phrase. Keep it simple. Any other actions you notice in the scene are important tactics that help you obtain your objective, but they are not the primary objective for the scene. A Scene Objective should be stated actively and succinctly so you can easily translate the objective into action. If you keep it simple and direct, you can remember it. Then, you can say it over and over in your head before you go into a scene, essentially willing it into action and influencing everything you do in the scene.

Are you still wondering what a strong Objective Statement might be for the scene mentioned previously? What if the Scene Objective was identified as *to gain her support for my study time tonight?* Let's test this Objective Statement with the **Scene Objective Checklist** that follows. This checklist can be used to test any Scene Objective.

Scene Objective Checklist

☐ Is it anchored in a basic human need?

☐ Does it focus on one single outcome?

☐ Does it utilize only one Action Word?

☐ Does it motivate your actions throughout the entire scene?

☐ Does it contribute to your character's Main Objective?

☐ Does it include the need for your scene partner's participation?

☐ Is it stated in positive terms, focusing on what you want, not what you don't want?

☐ Is it a short, single-subject phrase, stated in the first person?

☐ Does the desire for the outcome have great immediate urgency?

☐ Is the achievement of the outcome challenging but conceivable?

☐ Is there a specific victory that would end all actions toward this outcome?

Notice the Objective Statement, *to gain her support for my study time tonight*, includes: (1) a Cognitive need—to learn, (2) motivation for all the actions in the scene, (3) your friend's participation in the needs of the objective, (4) one active simple word—*to gain*, and (5) the implication of urgency stated in *tonight*. Depending on the specific victory you select for the scene, if your friend allows you to study for your test by either helping you, leaving you alone, or quietly supporting you by getting dinner and doing something else until you are done, then you will have a victory. An important lesson to learn in identifying your Scene Objective is this: Don't allow Action Tactics to mislead your identification of an active Scene Objective. Action Tactics are the tools for the job, not the goal of the job.

Questions to consider when investigating the script for objective clues:

1. What needs and desires does your character mention?

2. What do other characters say about your character's needs, desires, and activities?
3. What reactions does your character express when met with obstacles?
4. What actions does your character take that would reveal a common thread or goal?
5. What aspects of language, expressive behavior, and actions does your character exhibit that sets the character apart from others? Why?
6. How does the evidence found in your answers to questions 1-5 point toward one future desire, either immediate (Scene Objective), short term (Main Objective) or long term (Super Objective)?

Digging for Deeper Reasons

I sit puzzled as I watch an actor run around the stage in hot pursuit of Mrs. Saunders in Caryl Churchill's play Cloud Nine. *The actor playing Clive leers and paws at the attractive woman who is reluctantly seeking safety at his family's British Colony home in South Africa during a recent uprising. The actor is very active in his lusty pursuit of this woman whenever his wife and children are not looking; however, there appears to be something missing in how he pursues her. His actions don't seem to be motivated by anything more than the mere lust for an attractive woman.*

I ask the actor, "Why do you want Mrs. Saunders?" He responds with a wry smile, "She's hot! Can't that be enough of a reason?"

I tell the actor that his pursuit of Mrs. Saunders must be very different from how his friend, Harry pursues sex. I add, "Harry is having sex with nearly everyone, and Clive disapproves of Harry's actions. Why is Clive pursuing only Mrs. Saunders? And then when Clive's wife finds out about the affair and attacks Mrs. Saunders, why does Clive cast Mrs. Saunders away so easily?" The actor playing Clive looks at me with a blank stare and says, "I hadn't thought about all that."

I schedule a time when the actor and I can sit and talk about the details of Clive's motivations. I wonder—"Can I get him and the other actors to connect with deeper, more meaningful reasons for pursuing the multitude of sexual relationships presented in this play?" Later, I sit with the actors for a table discussion concerning their objectives for the sexual relationships in the play. I ask each to search through the list of basic human needs and align one of the basic needs with the reason they are seeking the relationships they pursue.

The actor playing Harry, the wild bachelor adventurer, decides that his character, who is without a societal attachment, uses his sexual advances with nearly everyone in Clive's household as attempts at finding belongingness. This Thought discovery helps the actor a great deal, particularly in understanding why his character pursues relations with Clive, as well as with Clive's young son, Edward.

The actress playing Mrs. Saunders investigates the character's lines and realizes that her reason for having an affair with Clive is Security. She is looking for a safe haven in the violent uprisings occurring in their British colony, and by satisfying Clive's desires for her, she can remain in the protection of his household, even though she does so with disdain, ultimately wanting to be on her own.

Finally, the actor playing Clive, after some detailed exploration of motivations, needs, and desires, realizes that he pursues Mrs. Saunders out of Ego needs. Clive is a British pioneer in the wild country of South Africa during the late 1800s. He has settled a colony there; he has an obedient family and a compliant soft wife who attends to his every need—but he needs more of a challenge to satisfy his Ego need as the adventurer and conqueror. Clive likes things wild and challenging, and he misses that spark in his life. Mrs. Saunders represents a wild mare who stomps about and insists on being free. Her feral behavior is erotically attractive to Clive's ego. He tries to reconnect with his own feral desires by having relations with her. When his wife ferociously attacks Mrs. Saunders in a knock-down-drag-out cat fight, Clive is tantalized by seeing this wild side of his wife. Re-attracted to her again, he can easily dismiss Mrs. Saunders.

Since this particularly adventurous actor is very willing to embody his characters, taking physical and emotional leaps easily and unabashedly, all he needed was a clear motivating source for those emotions and actions. Fueled with this new knowledge of Clive's thoughts and beliefs about his relationships with these two women, the *actor easily connected those thoughts with his actions and emotions. This allowed him to produce the strong, domineering, ego-centered character of Clive.*

Try This:

Watch a movie you have not seen before, and on a device where you can stop the action and take notes. During the opening scenes or exposition—where you might learn about the primary characters' objectives through their words and behavior—notice all the minor actions: eye contact with others, small tasks, treatment of objects, minor accommodations to others in conversation, basic body language, etc. To you, the witness, these actions are clues to the unfolding story, or little mysteries yet to be solved. To the actor playing the role, these are predominantly tactics the actor is using to achieve the character's objective. Make notes of these minor actions and, before you progress with the movie, try to determine the primary characters' objectives for the opening scenes and then for the entire movie. Then, watch the rest of the movie and learn what the characters were actually trying to achieve. See if their motivations match with your predictions.

The Super Objective

A character's Super Objective, or what he wants out of life, forms much of that character's identity. Consider some people you know well. Could you identify their Super Objectives? Do those objectives contribute to your perception of their identities and impressions on others? Are you basing your assumption of their Super Objective on knowledge of their past, as well as their present experiences? Most likely you are doing many of these things. Our back-stories, or life histories, contribute to our own as well as to others' perceptions of our identity and personality. The Super Objective captures this identity in a concise active statement, a base upon which you can build your character and his actions.

You can determine your character's Super Objective after you investigate the entire script, establishing the Main Objective as well as many Scene

Objectives. Key pieces of information about the character's past and present experiences, as well as clues to future aspirations, will be found in such an investigation. After this investigation, you will have a much clearer sense of what your character is saying and doing. You will also acquire a better view of the larger picture for your character's overall actions. A total view includes both what your character says and does, and what other characters throughout the play state about your character in the past, present, and future.

The Super Objective influences your character's personality, reputation, personal internal drive, and ability to make big decisions. In your own life, your ultimate goal may be *to own a restaurant, to win at my sport in the Olympics, to parent successful children, to achieve head cardiac surgeon status in a hospital,* or *to own a beautiful house with a large piece of property.* Whatever the life goal you may have, it will certainly reflect who you are, how you represent yourself to others, and what choices you make in your immediate and long-term plans.

Referring back to the exercise on visiting an old friend, can you see how the Super Objective might influence this simple scene if that old friend could be your future husband/wife and your Super Objective is *to parent successful children*? What if the old friend is an owner of a restaurant you hope to buy someday and your Super Objective is *to own a restaurant*? Your overriding life need, or Super Objective, would certainly influence your Scene Objective and your behavior in these examples.

Investigating the script thoroughly for clues about your character's wishes and dreams, ultimately creating his/her Super Objective, will then help you line up your Main Objective and Scene Objectives. The order of objective identification may vary from actor to actor. Depending on the actor's preferred method of reasoning, he may instinctively understand the character's Super Objective after the first read of a play, and then through deductive reasoning, go back and establish the Main and Scene Objectives. However, another actor may naturally use inductive reasoning, where she identifies the Scene Objectives first and then builds a case for the Main and Super Objectives. Regardless of the actor's investigative process (deductive vs. inductive), the clues are all in the script.

In addition to providing insight into the Main and Scene Objectives, determining the Super Objective will also help explain your character's behavior and bigger choices along the way. For example, imagine that your Super Objective is *to achieve head cardiac surgeon status in a hospital,* however you are working at a bank part-time simply to pay the bills while finishing your undergraduate degree. You are then offered a well-paid, full-time job in a bank, with the possibility of advancement professionally in the future. This offer comes while you are secretly struggling with entry exam studies for medical school. You turn down the job offer, because you know that taking the job would impede your long-range goals and interfere with your current studies. Others around you may not understand why you turned down the job if they don't know your Super Objective, but *you* do, and this knowledge was highly influential in the decision.

To identify the Super Objective for your character:

(1) Determine the Main Objective and a few Scene Objectives in the script.

(2) Make note of any personal wishes or dreams your character states or implies throughout the script.

(3) Look for common themes in the Main and Scene Objectives, and consider how they might point toward an overall life dream.

(4) Test your Super Objective Statement using the Super Objective Checklist.

Super Objective Checklist

☐ Is it anchored in a basic human need?

☐ Does it focus on one single outcome?

☐ Does it utilize only one Action Word?

☐ Does it motivate your actions throughout and well beyond the action of the script?

☐ Is it supported by your character's Main Objective?

☐ Is it stated in positive terms, focusing on what you want, not what you don't want?

☐ Is it a short, single-subject phrase, stated in the first person?

❏ Is the achievement of the outcome extremely difficult, taking nearly a lifetime to accomplish?

❏ Is there a specific victory that would end all actions toward this outcome?

Sample Super Objectives for Characters in *Proof*

The characters in the play *Proof* are Catherine, her sister Claire, their father Robert, and Robert's graduate student, Hal. Looking at these four characters, see if you can determine which Super Objective connects to each of these four characters.

1. To create, for my entire family, an enviable life in Manhattan (Ego need)

2. To establish myself world-wide as a top mathematician (Ego need)

3. To triumph over my perceived mental illness by publishing an extraordinary proof (Fulfillment need)

4. To awaken my genetic brilliance in my daughter (Spiritual need)

Try This:

After reading a play or watching a movie, summarize a character's actions, commentary, and decisions throughout the story and see if you can determine the character's Super Objective. Follow the guidelines listed for identifying a Super Objective. Then, work backwards and identify the character's Main Objective and a few Scene Objectives, using the checklists previously provided. Now, select a second character in the play or movie and reverse the order of your process. This time, work from Scene Objectives, to Main Objective, to Super Objective in your script analysis process for this character. Which process worked best for you? Either order of investigation works, often determined by the actor's procedural preferences (inductive vs. deductive reasoning) or the style of play or movie investigated.

Using Action Words

Once a need is identified, actions must be taken in order to satisfy that need. The Objective Statements each center on the primary action being pursued to satisfy the need. With this in mind, you must use strong action oriented words to articulate these goals. An Action Word describes something that you, someone, or something can actually do. Some might say to simply use action verbs. However, there are plenty of action verbs that are not strong choices for Action Words within Objective Statements. There are specific criteria for well-suited Action Words in Objective Statements. Also, for purposes of simplification, we will use the term Action Word in order to avoid any confusion over grammatical writing terms, such as passive and active verbs. *Action Word* will be used throughout this discussion as the overarching term for a word that represents action.

Strong Action Words for Objective Statements would be words that:

1. Have the potential to bring about a specific outcome

2. Focus the action on a direct recipient, or a person whose reactions will give evidence of a successful completion of the objective

3. Can be exhibited through external activities

4. Provide a range of actions, activities, and interactions with others

Some Weak vs. Strong Choices

Weak	*Strong*
To be	To get
To want	To make
To know	To convince

The words in the Weak Choices list (*to be, to want, to know*) connote contemplation, stillness, and passivity. Certainly, in life we often act on *wants* and yearn *to be* and *to know*. However, for purposes of creating dramatic action, an actor must make choices that imply strong actions, even within the language of their character analysis. The words in the Strong Choices list (*to get, to make, to convince*) could replace the weaker choices in order to create an Objective Statement that supports desired actions within an objective. These words imply external actions and interactions with others in order to achieve a desired outcome from someone or something. Always focus on the doing—the action.

Exercise
Rewording Objective Statements

Below are examples of weak Objective Statements. They are rooted in different basic needs but lack at least one of the recommended aspects of strong Objective Statements. First, identify what makes the following statements weak. Then reword each one making a strong active choice. Refer to the objective checklists for helpful guidelines. The first two examples have been answered. Can you complete the rest?

1. *I want to be loved*

This Objective Statement is a weak choice because this statement uses "to be" and does not include a focus for the action, like referring to the person from whom "I" wants love.

A stronger Objective Statement for this could be *to get him to confess that he loves me before our date ends.*

2. *To know I am intelligent*

This Objective Statement is a weak choice because this statement uses an internal choice of "to know" and does not include an external focus for the action, like basing the result on someone else.

A stronger Objective Statement for this could be *to get her to affirm my intelligence.*

3. *To be left alone*

This Objective Statement is a weak choice because

_____

A stronger Objective Statement for this could be

_____

4. *I don't want him to ask me out*

This Objective Statement is a weak choice because

_____

A stronger Objective Statement for this could be

_____

5. *I want to be rich and for him to marry me*

This Objective Statement is a weak choice because

_____

A stronger Objective Statement for this could be

_____

6. *To avoid being made fun of*

This Objective Statement is a weak choice because

_____

A stronger Objective Statement for this could be

_____

7. *To get her to sign her autograph on my program and agree to go out with me*

This Objective Statement is a weak choice because

_____

A stronger Objective Statement for this could be

_____

8. *To eat*

This Objective Statement is a weak choice because

_____

A stronger Objective Statement for this could be

_____

9. *To protect myself*

This Objective Statement is a weak choice because

_____

A stronger Objective Statement for this could be

_____

10. *I want to be beautiful*

This Objective Statement is a weak choice because

_____

A stronger Objective Statement for this could be

_____

Selecting Action Words

It can be challenging to find the active word most suitable for the Objective Statement. Here are two clear steps to make this process easier.

(1) Select an Action Word that implies a clear and finite outcome.

(2) Select an Action Word that relates to a basic need.

Additional Weak vs. Strong Choices

Weak	_Strong_
To exonerate	To free
To mock	To improve
To yell	To intimidate
To crave	To acquire

The first step, **select an Action Word that implies a clear and finite outcome**, refers to using words that point the action toward something that can be completed. For example the words: _acquire, seduce, guard, possess, solve, create, master,_ and _liberate_ all imply a victory within the very word choice. Won't you know when you have successfully guarded, acquired, possessed, mastered, or created something? The outcome of _seduction_ is obvious, and when one liberates or solves something, there is a clearly implied ending to the action. However, other word choices may not imply a clear ending or they may indicate infinite actions, such as _tantalize, bluff, grope, joke, mock, nurture, needle,_ and _try_. How do you know if you have gained something specific from a given situation by bluffing, joking, mocking, or nurturing? When wording an objective, your strongest choice for an Action Word is one that helps you see the potential for an ending to the action—a victory.

The second step in selecting an Action Word for your objective is to **(2) select an Action Word that relates to a basic need.** Since you already rooted your objective in a basic human need, keep going with this clear analytical process by matching a word that complements the need. If your basic need is the Body need sex, then a strong word match for this action is _to seduce._ However if your need is the Ego need recognition, then actions like _to prevail, to claim, to convince,_ and _to exploit_ would make excellent choices.

Types of Words to Avoid

Steer clear of words that are highly intellectual, emotional, or existential. Keep your word choices simple and easy to understand. If the word is too intellectual like, *to ruminate, to exonerate, to cogitate*, and so on, you could end up caught in a net of semantic deciphering, rather than simply applying a strong action. Don't try to apply emotional content to the objective with such actions as *to yell, to joke, to envy*, etc. This will limit your objective to one emotional tone or delivery. Later on in the script analysis, you will apply plenty of emotionally colorful words, or Emotion Tactics, that will guide your delivery. However, they do not belong in the overall objective. As noted previously, the use of *to be* is not advisable, as it comes across more existential in your interpretation, prompting the actor to internalize the objective inside his head. Other such existential words to avoid are *to wish, to want, to dream, to crave*, etc. None of these words prompt outward action, and instead merely focus on a need or desire without a clear way of getting it.

Action Words and Basic Needs

The following are eight basic human needs matched with Action Words that imply clear outcomes. Many of the words can be easily interchanged from one need to the next, so there is some repetition from list to list. The categorizing is meant as a general guide to help simplify the Action Word selection process. Do not consider these lists as ironclad boundaries or rules, but as supportive groupings. Refer to these words as a beginning guide for creating your Objective Statements.

Body Needs

To climax	To rejuvenate
To comfort	To repair
To cool	To satiate
To dry	To satisfy
To find	To seduce
To get	To take
To heal	To warm
To quench	

Thoughts

Security Needs

To avenge	To overcome
To break	To prepare
To capture	To protect
To cast off	To provide
To confront	To regain
To conquer	To restore
To escape	To secure
To establish	To shelter
To guard	To stabilize
To hold	

Social Needs

To acquire	To gain
To ally	To get
To beguile	To hold
To build	To keep
To celebrate	To lure
To charm	To obtain
To choose	To reject
To confess	To repair
To conspire	To seduce
To convince	To select
To co-operate	To soothe
To establish	To strengthen
To find	

Ego Needs

To accomplish	To gain
To achieve	To intimidate
To attain	To make
To bury	To persuade
To captivate	To possess
To claim	To prevail
To complete	To recommend
To convince	To regain
To defend	To save
To distinguish	To seize
To dominate	To undermine
To exploit	To win

Cognitive Needs

To acquire	To mold
To build	To plan
To challenge	To predict
To decipher	To prepare
To define	To probe
To earn	To quell
To expose	To search
To fix	To solve
To gain	To teach
To guide	To uncover
To infuse	To unmask
To learn	

Beauty Needs

To acquire	To generate
To afford	To increase
To beautify	To inspire
To captivate	To make
To cherish	To obtain
To create	To prove
To decorate	To purchase
To enhance	To relish
To expand	To satisfy
To fashion	To take
To gain	

Fulfillment Needs

To accomplish	To pull off
To achieve	To reach
To conquer	To regain
To discover	To reveal
To dominate	To rule
To fulfill	To satisfy
To implement	To succeed
To lead	To surmount
To master	To trap
To overcome	To triumph
To prevail	

Spiritual Needs

To allow	To inspire
To arouse	To liberate
To awaken	To motivate
To celebrate	To open
To embrace	To release
To enlighten	To seek
To enthuse	To share
To free	To trust
To honor	

Sample Objective Statements

Here is a list of Objective Statements using the process described previously. Each objective is motivated by a basic human need and utilizes an Action Word that implies an outcome.

Body Need

To rejuvenate my energy with a game of tennis

To reach a climax with her at the same time

To warm us up before we perish from the cold

To satiate my relentless hunger for his coveted truffles

To find a comfortable place to rest our weary bodies

Security Need

To stabilize our boat so we don't capsize

To restore order by ending their feud

To conquer my assailant

To escape from his territorial reign

To avenge my father's death

Thoughts

Social Need

To ally with her so we can work well together

To gain his regard for my mothering skills

To charm her into marrying me

To confess my weaknesses to my insecure husband

To build a trust with her

Ego Need

To seize control of this disorganized business meeting

To save her from her pitiful debts

To exploit the band under my company's title

To bury my sordid past far from his knowledge

To achieve a prestigious position in his company

Cognitive Need

To solve the riddle in our treasure hunt

To challenge his logic

To earn a good grade on our project

To quell her fears of technology

To predict the inevitable outcome of his weak plan

Beauty Need

To afford our overextended vacation

To enhance his looks with a few changes

To increase my home's value with her landscaping skills

To inspire him to play in our band

To captivate him with my new look

Ultimate Fulfillment Need

To surmount my formidable opponent

To implement my superior plan for the company

To reach the finish line before everyone else

To triumph with my family at the end of this long feud

To accomplish my greatest work, ever

Spiritual Need

To open their hearts to salvation

To inspire a winning attitude in my team

To release my doubts of external forces

To allow my thoughts and actions to reflect a higher purpose

To trust in the laws of the universe

Exercise
Build an Objective Statement

Here are brief descriptions of scenes from plays or movies. See whether you can determine a Scene Objective for each. Use Maslow's Hierarchy of Needs and match those needs with Action Words from the Action Words lists. Write the objective as if you were playing the role—in first person point of view.

1. **A man** and his younger girlfriend wait in a cosmetic surgeon's waiting room. He is there because his girlfriend suggested he get a nose job. While they wait for his call, he jokes about nose jobs and how absurd they are, he mentions how other handsome men have big noses, he talks about how great their relationship is right now, and he offers to show her a tattoo he had done for her.

Basic Need_____

Action Word_____

Scene Objective_____

2. **A woman** who shares her home with her elderly mother busies herself around the house urgently organizing her mother's medication schedule, her favorite foods and phone numbers of people to call for anything she might need, and reminding her where everything is in the house. She also asks her mother if she knows where the handgun is kept. The woman acts with determination and focuses on the details like a shopping list. By the end of the scene the woman tells her mother, very matter-of-factly, that she wants to spend a nice day with her but then this evening she will commit suicide by shooting herself.

Basic Need_____

Action Word_____

Scene Objective_____

3. **A boxer** with a wife and three children living during the Depression Era has no money to pay for electricity, food, or heat and his children are starving and getting sick from such conditions. His wife sent the children off to distant family members in order to protect them from the elements, but he vowed they would all stay together, no matter what happened. In this scene, he goes to a men's club where wealthy businessmen, who used to benefit from his winning fights, are enjoying afternoon drinks and smokes. He humbles himself before them, publicly announces his predicament, and asks for assistance.

Basic Need_____

Action Word_____

Scene Objective_____

4. **A woman** who has lost almost everything she had and is living in her sister's cramped apartment desperately needs to feel like her former self again. It is a very hot day, and the entire environment from the neighborhood to the apartment is fully distasteful to her. Despite her brother-in-law's complaints of her lengthy time in the bathroom and use

of water, she takes a long bath, dresses in her best dress, reminisces about old times when she had many admirers, and does her hair.

Basic Need_____

Action Word_____

Scene Objective_____

5. **A senior martial artist** is asked to teach his superior skills to a boy being harassed by very dangerous young martial artists. However, the elderly man sees that the boy is impatient and at times disrespectful of the disciplined process required to learn such a skill. So when the boy arrives for a lesson, the man gives him tasks to do around the house like painting his fence and washing and waxing his car. Whenever the boy questions the task or asks when they will begin karate lessons, the man calmly reminds him of the task at hand and how to do it well. Unbeknownst to the soon enraged boy, the elderly man is helping him gain valuable muscle, balance, and movement skills by completing these very simple tasks.

Basic Need_____

Action Word_____

Scene Objective_____

6. **A young woman** has a brother who has fallen to his death while leading a bloody siege against their city and king. The king decides to make an example of her brother's crime and display the consequences to anyone who attempts to do the same. The king forbids anyone to bury the brother, leaving him to rot in the street. He further decrees that anyone who tries to bury him will be publicly stoned to death. In the scene, the young woman meets secretly with her sister and tells her of her plan to bury her brother. The woman reminds her sister it is a worse crime against the Gods and the spirit of her brother to leave him unburied and without ceremony. The woman begs her sister to help

her. When her sister declines with fear, the woman rebukes her with anger and bravely states she will attempt it herself.

Basic Need_____

Action Word_____

Scene Objective_____

7. **An older man** who has led a prestigious life in the world of mathematics is struggling with dementia. In his more lucid moments, he recognizes that his days may be numbered and so he dedicates all his time to working on math problems. Day and night he fills notebooks with problems, believing he is on the brink of making his greatest discovery yet. In this scene his daughter comes home to visit, worried for his health and well-being. He has reached a point in his work that he feels is particularly remarkable and is so absorbed in the work that he doesn't even notice the cold as he writes outside in the winter weather. He tells his daughter of his groundbreaking discovery and asks her to read it. He watches her intently as she reacts with confusion while she reads his findings.

Basic Need_____

Action Word_____

Scene Objective_____

8. **An aristocratic woman** returns from her long honeymoon to a new house her husband purchased for them, thinking it would make her happy. She is bored with her husband, unhappy with the new house, and dreading the thought of soon being a mother. In this scene the husband's aunt comes to visit, focusing her attention on the husband, his writings, and his potential for a new position at a university. The aunt also learns that the aristocratic woman is pregnant and promises to come by regularly to check on the future family. The aristocratic woman treats the aunt coldly while the aunt dotes on their new home. At one point, the

woman complains that one of the maids left her old hat on a chair, knowing full well it was the aunt's hat.

Basic Need_____

Action Word_____

Scene Objective_____

Exercise
Creating Victory Statements

Using the eight scenes described previously in the **Build an Objective Statement** exercise, build on the Scene Objectives you created for these scenes and write a Victory Statement for each. Refer to the **Victory Statement Checklist** as a guide.

1. **A man** and his younger girlfriend wait in a cosmetic surgeon's waiting room before he is to get a nose job.

   Scene Objective_____

   Victory Statement_____

2. **A woman** who shares her home with her elderly mother busies herself around the house, urgently organizing her mother's things.

   Scene Objective_____

   Victory Statement_____

3. **A boxer** with a wife and three children during the Depression Era confronts his rich colleagues at the men's club.

   Scene Objective_____

   Victory Statement_____

4. **A woman** who has lost almost everything she had and is living in her sister's cramped apartment takes a long bath and beautifies herself despite her brother-in-law's complaints.

Scene Objective_____

Victory Statement_____

5. **A senior martial artist** in the process of teaching a boy karate gives him tasks to do around the house, like painting his fence and washing and waxing his car.

Scene Objective_____

Victory Statement_____

6. **A young woman** meets secretly with her sister and tells her of her plan to bury their dead brother, which is against the king's command.

Scene Objective_____

Victory Statement_____

7. **An older man** tells his daughter of his groundbreaking mathematical discovery and asks her to read his notes to confirm the news.

Scene Objective_____

Victory Statement_____

8. **An aristocratic woman** treats her new husband's aunt coldly and complains that one of the maids left her old hat on a chair, knowing full well it was the aunt's hat.

Scene Objective_____

Victory Statement_____

Summary of Objective Use

Let us return to the question raised at the beginning of this chapter: "If the bare essence of acting with someone in a scene is to know why your character stays in a room with another character, then what keeps your character in the room? Why not leave?" You now know that placing your focus on obtaining a highly desirous outcome from the other in the scene is the answer.

Looking further into this simple example of scene study, we also know that the key to good dramatic action is conflict. We can then surmise that once a person gets what they want, the conflict is over. So throughout the scene, the characters would be met with obstacles preventing them from getting what they want.

The Basis of Every Scene: Give it to me!/No!

We can boil down most any scene or story into a very basic subtext pattern. By doing so you can reveal the roots of basic needs, thoughts, and actions. For example, consider the classic children's folktale, *The Three Little Pigs*. In this story, a wolf continuously visits the homes of three different pigs and asks to be let in, with the need-based objective, *to eat*. The pigs always say, "No" with their need-based objective, *to remain safe*. The pigs want the wolf to respect the boundaries of their homes that keep them safe, but the wolf denies that request with his continued pursuit to enter. The wolf and the pigs each attempt many different tactics throughout the story to achieve their individual objectives. The basic pattern of subtext for nearly every scene is for each character to demand what they need and for the opposing force to keep providing a denial. A scene that is rooted in need-based objectives, and encounters obstacles throughout, could be shown by the following simple dialogue of basic thoughts between characters A and B:

A: Give it to me.

B: No.

B: Give it to me.

A: No.

(Etc. until someone says "Yes" or someone gives up on this particular objective.)

Exercise
Improvised Scene with Give it to me!/No!

In groups of two do the following:

1. Decide on a basic scenario of relationship and place for the two people in this scene. For example, two sisters meeting up in the park, two friends at a reunion in a hotel ballroom, two strangers in a diner, etc.

2. Take eight index cards and write one of the needs from Maslow's Hierarchy on each of the cards. *(e.g. card one is Body needs—hunger, thirst, sleep, sex, physical comfort, and card two is Security needs—shelter, order, law and governance, limits, stability, etc.)*

3. Shuffle the cards, and with them face down, each partner selects one card and keeps the content a secret from each other.

4. Each person creates an objective based on the need they selected and the relationship and place decision made by the two. Partners keep their needs and objectives a secret from the other.

5. Stand some distance apart with backs turned to each other. Close your eyes and conduct an impromptu Doorway Visualization for the scene, based on this need and objective. How do you hope it will play out? What is your desired victory?

6. When ready, turn around and face your partner. In your mind, say your objective over and over again as you interact with your partner. Allow this internal thought to manifest in your actions, behaviors, body language, and emotions as you interact with your partner. Even if your partner has not turned around yet, when you see your partner's back you can connect these thoughts to your behavior as you recognize that the person before you can provide you with your victory.

7. Engage with your partner in a form of improvised scene, based mainly in behavior supported by this one need and objective. If you need words, the only dialogue possible from either person is "Give it to me" and "No." Allow the very nature of your delivery of these lines to project how you feel, what you need, what you want, and how you react to your thoughts

as well as your partner's actions and words.

8. Try not to resort to guessing games or pantomime simply to get your partner to guess your need. Engage your own truth and belief in your need and objective and allow your behaviors to embody these thoughts. Be sure to react to what happens to you, by you, and through you.

9. If you are in a larger group of actors, do this exercise in groups of four, allowing the other two in the group to serve as observers who give feedback after the scene is over. Can the observers identify the needs and objectives present in the scene? Then, do the exercise again with the observers now creating a new scene, using steps 1-8 in this exercise.

Exercise
Identifying the Give it to me!/No! in Scripted Scenes

Looking back at the eight example scenes provided in this chapter, can you see in each one this simple pattern underneath the details of its circumstances?

(1) *The Shape of Things*
A man and his younger girlfriend wait in a cosmetic surgeon's waiting room. He is there because his girlfriend suggested he get a nose job. While they wait for his call, he jokes about nose jobs and how absurd they are, he mentions how other handsome men have big noses, he talks about how great their relationship is right now, and he offers to show her a tattoo he had done for her.

1. A man's "Give it to me" is his desire to gain his girlfriend's acceptance as he appears now.
2. He receives "No" from his girlfriend as she insists on the nose surgery.
3. The girlfriend's "Give it to me" is her desire to change him.
4. She receives "No" from him as he provides examples of others who are considered handsome with big noses.

Thoughts

(2) *'Night Mother*

A woman who shares her home with her elderly mother busies herself around the house, urgently organizing her mother's medication schedule, her favorite foods, and phone numbers of people to call for anything she might need, and reminding her where everything is in the house. She also asks her mother if she knows where the handgun is kept. The woman acts with determination and focuses on the details like a shopping list. By the end of the scene the woman tells her mother, very matter-of-factly, that she wants to spend a nice day with her, but then this evening she will commit suicide by shooting herself.

1. A woman's "Give it to me" is her need for proof that her elderly dependent mother will survive on her own after the young woman's suicide.
2. She receives "No" from her mother creates ways to stall her daughter's suicide.
3. The mother's "Give it to me" is her need to convince her daughter that there is a reason to live.
4. The mother receives "No" responses as the daughter explains all the reasons she has for wanting to end it all.

(3) *Cinderella Man*

A boxer, with a wife and three children living during the Depression Era, has no money to pay for electricity, food or heat and his children are starving and getting sick from such conditions. His wife sent the children off to distant family members in order to protect them from the elements, but he vowed they would stay together no matter what happened. In this scene, he goes to a men's club where wealthy businessmen, who used to benefit from his winning fights, are enjoying afternoon drinks and smokes. He humbles himself before them, publicly announces his predicament, and asks for assistance.

1. A boxer's "Give it to me" is to get financial help from the wealthy men at the club.
2. He receives "No" from the men's initial silence and distain for his begging.
3. The men's "Give it to me" is their need for this man to resolve his problem.

on his own so they don't have to face the truth of the recession's impact.

4. The men receive a "No" from the boxer as he refuses to leave until they help him.

Continue This Exercise On Your Own

See if you can fill in the "Give it to me" motivations and "No" reactions for the following situations. Ideally you would read these plays or watch these movies before completing this exercise in order to fully understand the characters and scenes being described in their short forms below. However, many assumptions of basic human behavioral needs and scene conflicts can already be made within the general scenarios described.

(4) *A Streetcar Named Desire*

A woman who has lost almost everything she had and is living in her sister's cramped apartment desperately needs to feel like her former self again. It is a very hot day, and the entire environment from the neighborhood to the apartment is fully distasteful to her. Despite her brother-in-law's complaints of her lengthy time in the bathroom and use of water, she takes a long bath, dresses in her best dress, reminisces of old times when she had many admirers, and does her hair.

1. A woman's "Give it to me" is_____

2. She receives "No" from _____

3. The man's "Give it to me" is_____

4. The man receives "No" from_____

(5) *The Karate Kid*

A senior martial artist is asked to teach his superior skills to a boy being harassed by very dangerous young martial artists. However, the elderly man sees that the boy is impatient and at times disrespectful of the disciplined process required to learn such a skill. So when the boy arrives for a lesson, the man gives him tasks to do around the house like painting his fence and washing and waxing his car. Whenever the boy questions the task or asks when they will begin karate lessons, the man calmly reminds him of the task at hand and how to do it well. Unbeknownst to the soon enraged boy, the elderly man is helping the boy gain valuable muscle, balance, and movement skills by completing these very simple tasks.

1. The teacher's "Give it to me" is_____

2. He receives "No" from _____

3. The boy's "Give it to me" is_____

4. The boy receives "No" from_____

(6) *Antigone*

A young woman has a brother who has fallen to his death while leading a bloody siege against their city and king. The king decides to make an example of her brother's crime and display the consequences to anyone who attempts to do the same. The king forbids anyone to bury the brother, leaving him to rot in the street. He further decrees that anyone who tries to bury him will be publicly stoned to death. In the scene, the young woman meets secretly with her sister and tells her of her plan to bury her brother. The woman reminds her sister it is a worse crime against the Gods and the spirit of her brother to leave him unburied and without ceremony. The woman begs her sister to help her. When her sister declines with fear, the woman rebukes her with anger and bravely states she will attempt it herself.

1. A young woman's "Give it to me" is_____

2. She receives "No" from _____

3. The sister's "Give it to me" is_____

4. The sister receives "No" from_____

(7) *Proof*

An older man who has led a prestigious life in the world of mathematics is struggling with dementia. In his more lucid moments he recognizes that his days may be numbered and so he dedicates all his time to working on math problems. Day and night he fills notebooks with problems, believing he is on the brink of making his greatest discovery yet. In this scene his daughter comes home to visit, worried for his health and well-being. He has reached a point in his work that he feels is particularly remarkable and is so absorbed in the work that he doesn't even notice the cold as he writes outside in the winter weather. He tells his daughter of his groundbreaking discovery and asks her to read it. He watches her intently as she reacts with confusion while she reads his findings.

1. The father's "Give it to me" is_____

2. He receives "No" from _____

3. The daughter's "Give it to me" is_____

4. The daughter receives "No" from_____

(8) *Hedda Gabler*

An aristocratic woman returns from her long honeymoon to a new house her husband purchased for them, thinking it would make her happy. She is bored with her husband, unhappy with the new house, and dreading the thought of soon being a mother. In this scene the husband's aunt comes to visit, focusing her attention on the husband, his writings, and his potential for a new position at a university. The aunt also learns that the aristocratic woman is pregnant and promises to come by regularly to check on the future family. The aristocratic woman treats the aunt coldly while the aunt dotes on their new home. At one point, the woman complains that one of the maids left her old hat on a chair, knowing full well it was the aunt's hat.

1. An aristocratic woman's "Give it to me" is_____

2. She receives "No" from _____

3. The aunt's "Give it to me" is_____

4. The aunt receives "No" from_____

Thoughts and the Give it to me!/No!

Look at any scene you are currently rehearsing or have rehearsed in the past. Can you break this scene down into this simple pattern of "Give it to me" and "No"? Can you recognize that dramatic action is based around the following: (1) a character in need, who acts on that need by (2) devising a plan to obtain (3) something specific from others ("Give it to me") in order to satisfy that need; however, they don't easily obtain the thing they pursue because they are constantly (4) met with obstacles ("No"), and so they (5) attempt many actions and behaviors in order to obtain the thing they desire.

In acting terminology these five areas are as follows:

(1) Need

(2) Objective

(3) Victory

(4) Obstacles

(5) Tactics

Applying a Thought Approach

If you would like to use a Thought Approach as the MVP for your acting, follow these steps:

1. Read and investigate the entire script for clues to your character's needs and objectives from scene to scene.

2. Determine the need and objective for each scene, for the entire script, and for your character's life (Scene, Main, and Super Objectives).

3. Determine a specific victory for each objective.

4. Write an objective and Victory Statement for each Scene, Main, and Super Objective.

5. Go over all the checklists for Objective and Victory Statements to check your final work.

6. Rehearse your scenes applying the following exercises: Doorway Visualization and Give it to me!/No!

7. Invite a Side Coach to watch and remind you of your objectives, victories, and beat shift subtext *(see Emotions and Manifestation Chapters for more information on side coaching and beat shift subtext).*

8. Once the scene is memorized and rehearsed several times with the Thought approach, check to see that aspects of action and emotion have also clearly manifested in your performance. If not, apply exercises and techniques from those chapters to help bring these elements into your acting work.

Summary of Thoughts

Thoughts influence a character's needs, objectives, desired victories, obstacles, and tactics. As you read further and learn about the other elements of the TEAM, see if you can continue to recognize how these elements are explored and expressed through the other aspects of the TEAM. Remember that all parts of the TEAM are intrinsically tied together as mutual and reciprocal parts of a whole, supporting a fully-embodied acting process.

Further Study

Constantine Stanislavski was the first acting teacher to clearly identify and explain an acting method based in psychological theories and script analysis of objectives, obstacles, and tactics. Many techniques developed after Stanislavski's original developments are still based in his original theories. These core texts by Stanislavski will provide additional information as well as a glimpse at the original sources of these terms.

1. *An Actor Prepares* by Constantine Stanislavski

2. *The Stanislavski System* by Sonia Moore

3. *Respect for Acting* by Uta Hagen

Thoughts

For further information on Maslow's Hierarchy of Needs and their motivations for human interactions:

1. *Towards a Psychology of Being* by Abraham Maslow

2. *Motivation and Personality* by Abraham Maslow

"*If the water of the river is turbulent,*

the words will come out like a canoe

on a rough river. It all depends on the

flow of the river which is your emotion.

The text takes on the character

of your emotion."

– Sanford Meisner

Chapter 3

Emotions

Emotion *(noun): the affective aspect of consciousness: a state of feeling; a conscious mental reaction subjectively experienced usually directed toward something and typically accompanied by physiological and behavioral changes in the body. Etymology: from Middle French,* emouvoir *"to stir up" and Latin,* e-movere *"to-move."*[15]

There is a popular saying in the acting field, "50% of acting is reacting." This statement holds a great deal of truth when you consider human behavior is motivated not only by our thoughts, but by our feelings. If we had no feelings we would be mere automatons. Our emotions are what connect us with humanity, provide the social glue to our relationships, and mark our behaviors with truth or untruth. The definition of emotion refers to *a conscious mental reaction, usually directed toward something and typically accompanied by physiological and behavioral changes in the body.* Keeping this definition in mind, emotions are displayed by the way we react to situations, the feelings we express with our words and actions, and how these feelings are reflected in our stance, gestures, behaviors, and tactics. An individual's style of embodying these actions and reactions could be considered their personality. A person's manner of moving through space, interacting with others, speaking, gesturing, and even thinking is all colored by emotion.

15. "The Online Etymology Dictionary," accessed September 1, 2012, http://www.etymonline.com.

A famous study by UCLA Psychology Professor, Albert Mehrabian, discovered that when a person is expressing her thoughts about feelings and attitudes, the actual words she spoke had only 7% out of 100% impact on her audience; the rest of the impact was from nonverbal communication (body language 55% and tone of voice 38%).[16] Mehrabian's study is often referred to as the 7/38/55 rule. Another study from the British Journal of Social and Clinical Psychology found that all nonverbal cues had 4.3 times the impact than verbal cues (or an 81%/19% split).[17] These studies support the idea that our tone of voice and body language, which are the primary channels of emotional expression, have a greater impact on our audiences than the actual words we speak.

As you read on and learn more about how emotions affect acting, consider this: If your words and actions were devoid of emotion, how interesting would your performance be? If two actors were facing each other, repeating the "Give it to me" and "No" sequence from the end of the Thoughts chapter, would you notice differences in each actor's delivery of this simple sequence? You certainly would. The essence of those differences is emotion.

Emotional Colors and Emotion Tactics

Emotional Colors and Emotion Tactics are terms I developed over the years of forming the TEAM Approach to help actors differentiate between the conscious and unconscious uses of emotions. Emotional Colors are the unconscious and instinctive emotions exhibited through moods, feelings, habitual reactions, or states of being. Have you ever heard of someone being referred to as having a colorful personality? In life, our Emotional Colors are considered our personality, resulting from a lifetime of character building. In acting, the Emotional Colors displayed by a character are the results of the actor's work and preparation.

Emotion Tactics are conscious and intentionally chosen emotional approaches for, or reactions to, a situation. Consider times when you might have coached yourself as you approached someone with a difficult subject, or controlled your emotional reaction to a surprising situation. You were most likely using Emotion Tactics. You were consciously selecting emotional actions and reactions to better suit the situation. Young children can perfect Emotion Tactics. They learn this

16. Albert Mehrabian, Silent Messages, First Edition (California: Wadsworth, 1971), 75-80.
17. Michael Argyle, Veronica Salter, Hilary Nicholson, Marylin Williams, Philip Bergess, "The Communication of Inferior and Superior Attitudes by Verbal and Non-verbal Signals," British Journal of Social and Clinical Psychology, (1970) Volume 9, Issue 3, 222-231.

technique before they are able to speak, as they recognize how their emotional behavior creates specific reactions from adults. They then adopt Emotion Tactics to achieve what they need or want from adults. As children grow up, this ability becomes more refined, so refined many of us don't realize we are doing it anymore.

We regularly experience both unconscious Emotional Colors and conscious Emotion Tactics as we behave in our habitual states of being, or personality, and yet adjust for specific occasions such as an interview, personal introduction, or date. When an actor is first preparing a role, both types of emotional behavior for the character should be addressed.

Examining the script carefully for evidence of emotional behavior will help you identify your character's Emotional Colors and Tactics. After studying the text, you can apply emotions to character embodiment, personality, reactions, and Action Tactics. Once these initial decisions are made and practiced in early rehearsals, you may find yourself in flow, or at a place where you have obtained a somatic, or physically instinctive, understanding of your character's behavior. At that point you will find you can go in and out of conscious and unconscious emotional actions and reactions automatically, while staying true to your character's emotional foundation. This is a highly desirous rehearsal and performance state, when an actor has integrated intentional preparation work with spontaneous interactions to the character's given circumstances.

Intentional Emotion Scoring vs. Spontaneous Reactions

Some acting theories focus primarily on the character's actions, stressing use of objectives and stating, "Emotions will result from the strong pursuance of objectives." Emotions will result from this approach, often in the form of unconscious Emotional Colors. Many more will emerge when Emotion Tactics, clearly aligned with the character's thoughts and actions, are applied. Some actors have said, "I don't intentionally apply emotions to my work; I focus on the actions." What they may not realize is action is filled with emotion, and emotions are active. Emotion is so misunderstood in the acting field, often interpreted as big and self-indulgent acts on stage. Although present and obvious in those moments, emotion is also inherent in our habitual facial expressions, posture, stride, gestures, and nonverbal vocal reactions. Emotion creates inflection patterns in our speech, influences muscle tension, and changes our breathing patterns. The basic etymology of the word emotion—*e-movere* "to-move"—

implies action or a movement starting from within and radiating out. The actor who states he is not applying emotion to his acting, is actually exhibiting layers of emotion; however, such denial indicates he does so without fully knowing all aspects of his expressive behavior.

You are going to be much more in control of your craft if you recognize how emotion and expression are exhibited through you and your character. Otherwise your acting could result in unintentional behavior, a vulnerability to inconsistencies, too much reliance on inspiration, and lack of control. Since our feelings heavily influence behavior, it is essential to learn *how* your character behaves, when in action. The acting teacher Michael Chekhov refers to this "how" as the Quality. The quality of action includes the feelings of the character infused in actions. You must learn to become aware of this emotional quality in your acting work and *how* you can use it both as an intentional acting tool (Emotion Tactic) and as an integrative behavioral element (Emotional Color). It is also important to recognize how it rises up from your own personal behavior and can either support or contradict the role you are playing.

 ## *Emotionally Daring Monologue*

I am working as the Emotion Coach for a community performance project where the script is created by stories provided by community members and culled by a playwright into a series of monologues, scenes, and songs with a unifying theme. Some of the actors in the performance are people who contributed stories to the production, and I am working with one such actor, helping her prepare her monologue for performance.

The actor is a thoughtful and sensitive writer who contributed an analytically poetic coming-out story of her new identity. Years before, she was someone else, but now she stands before the audience, proudly staking her claim as transformed anew. We have already talked about the monologue and identified the Emotional Colors and Tactics shifting throughout. However, as she rehearses the piece, I see her physically retreating up stage, behind furniture, and even stepping back and sinking down in her posture in all the moments that we have identified as her being proud, courageous, feisty, and brazen. After reminding her a few times to address these conscious Emotion Tactics, and seeing her fall back in fear and sink down into sadness in each of these moments, I consider the possibility that her own fears and sadness from her personal past, being the writer of this monologue, might be preventing her from living the present active choices of the piece.

I ask her to stop and I point out these defaulting moments of fear and sadness. Tears well up in her eyes as she recognizes that she was thinking in those moments, "What will people think of me?" She is well aware that she is taking a bold step with her story and her performance, and her own fear of daring to proclaim this to the public is keeping her from fulfilling the truly bold statement she wants to deliver as the performer.

I suggest that she consciously override these moments with strong, aggressive Emotion Tactics, and I help her embody them so that her posture will not do one thing, and her thoughts another. We run the monologue a few times, and I call out to her, like a coach, in the moments we identified for her to step into her power. At first she has some minor impulses to shrink back, but after a few drills where she essentially reconditions her response and is cheered on by my reminders of her own choices, she succeeds. Through this process of raising awareness, skill building, and practice, she manages to match what the actor desires in her performance, with what the individual person can provide.

This actor was eventually able to embody this monologue with sensitivity and courage during each performance, which captured the empathy of many audience members.

Attaching Emotions to Action Words

How often have you heard someone say, "It's not what you say, it's *how* you say it" or "I don't like the *way* you did that"? These examples are common sayings stemming from our natural whole-self reading of human behavior and our observations of inconsistencies between words and expression. When someone comments on how you said something, they are referring to the emotional tone accompanying your words.

The chapter on Thoughts addressed how to identify Action Words for accurately leading an actor toward a desired result. It is important to realize that these Action Words can be colored with emotion to clarify the Quality, or expressive behavior.

[**Example**] Look at the following sentences:

A. "Don't forget to pick me up after work."

B. "That looks great on you."

C. "You don't need to pay me back."

You might assign the following Action Words to these sentences: (A) to remind, (B) to flatter, and (C) to dismiss. There are many ways you can remind, flatter, and dismiss.

Consider attaching these words to the actions: (A) to remind condescendingly, (B) to flatter jealously, and (C) to dismiss angrily.

While standing, imagine there is a person in front of you and say these statements, believing that you are doing and feeling the actions and qualities that the words in the parentheses imply.

"Don't forget to pick me up after work." (remind condescendingly)

"That looks great on you." (flatter jealously)

"You don't need to pay me back." (dismiss angrily)

By attaching words that imply emotions, feelings, and qualities to the Action Words, can you sense a change in your vocal tone and delivery? Do you also feel any changes in your posture, gestures, and facial expressions? Let's look at some other choices for the same actions:

"Don't forget to pick me up after work." (remind tenderly)

"That looks great on you." (flatter flirtatiously)

"You don't need to pay me back." (dismiss sadly)

When delivering the same statement, yet embodying different Emotion Tactics, can you detect a difference in your expressive behavior? Can you also imagine the possible changes in reactions from those receiving your varying deliveries?

Your actions, Emotion Tactics, and then the reactions of your scene partner are the intricate layers desired in dramatic action. Sanford Meisner compares the actor's use of emotions with text to a canoe on a river. Imagine the text as a canoe being jostled about by the river's currents, or the emotions. "If the water of the river is turbulent, the words will come out like a canoe on a rough river. It all depends on the flow of the river which is your emotion. The text takes on the character of your emotion."[18]

The most basic interpersonal communication includes a four-layer process.

1. We interpret information received by our surroundings.

2. We then establish feelings about these interpretations.

3. We convey these feelings through behavior and vocal tones.

4. We also establish feelings about how the communication was expressed.

We are highly complex beings with multiple levels of thoughts and thousands of emotions to experience and express to others. This complexity is clear when a person gets frustrated after crying in the midst of trying to express angry feelings, or feels guilty after laughing at something, or is ashamed about a fearful reaction. These feelings about feelings add to our emotional complexity.

Recognition of this intricate interpersonal exchange is essential to understanding your portrayal of a character and interactions with others. Utilizing the range and depth of expressive behavior will only strengthen and diversify your acting abilities.

Building Your Emotion Vocabulary

There are plenty of actors in the professional world who fine-tuned their craft of Emotional Coloring and tactic use through years of experience and good training. However, there are also many actors who are mystified by the process or may feel pigeon-holed in their acting work because they have not gained the ability to apply varied and dynamic emotional choices. For the latter, this book breaks down the emotion work into tangible elements that anyone can apply to acting. With regular practice and application of these techniques, this skill can become habitual.

18. Meisner, *Sanford Meisner on Acting*, 115.

It is important to build a vocabulary of emotionally colored words, which will eventually manifest into a wide range of expressive behavior. The larger your emotional vocabulary, the more expressive variety possible in your acting. If you search through a dictionary for words that express feelings, you will easily come across over 2,000 words. With so many options available for emotion scoring, you will want to narrow these choices down and select strong, distinctive words that guide you toward active embodiment. I recommend you organize them into general categories of basic emotions. This will make them quickly accessible and reflect the building blocks of emotion theory. An example of words within this type of categorization follows after the explanation of basic emotions.

Basic Emotions

Emotions, or words that imply feelings, can be categorized under primary or basic emotions. Psychologists and researchers support the theory that emotions can be categorized into a small number of basics or primaries. The primary emotions are felt and expressed on varying levels, or degrees. For example, pure anger expressed in low levels can convey irritation, aggravation, and annoyance. Higher levels communicate being furious, irate, hostile, or hateful.

The number of basic emotions identified within the varying theories vary greatly, from as few as two primaries to as many as ten. Some of the words used for these basic building blocks are Acceptance, Anger, Anticipation, Aversion, Disgust, Sensuality, Fear, Happiness, Pleasure, Sadness, Shame, Surprise, Tenderness, and Wonder. We will use the six Alba Emoting basic emotions to categorize emotionally colored words, since the Alba Emoting technique also provides a reliable scientifically proven technique for embodying these emotional states.

Mixed Emotions

All other emotions, beyond the varying levels of primaries, are mixes from these basics. For example, basic Anger, can mix with other emotions to create frustration (anger/sadness), envy (sensuality/anger), sarcasm (happiness/anger), pride (tenderness/anger), and disdain (anger/fear). At first glance, you may question, or even deny, the presence of some emotions identified within these mixes. Mixes can be quite subjective, particularly depending on how you personally feel about and convey these emotions. This only continues to support how highly complex and subjective human emotion can be.

Emotion Categories

The fundamental emotions in Alba Emoting are Anger, Sensuality[19], Fear, Happiness, Sadness, and Tenderness. What follows, are lists of emotionally-colored words categorized with these six basics.

Basic emotions can be expressed in many levels, and although a person may be expressing a basic emotion, society assigns many different words that capture the feelings of these low, mid, or high levels of the basic emotion.

[Examples]

A low level of (1) Anger, (2) Sensuality, (3) Fear, and (4) Sadness could be (1) insistent, (2)nostalgic, (3) shy, and (4) brooding.

A mid level of (1) Anger, (2) Sensuality, (3) Fear, and (4) Sadness could be (1) annoyed, (2) enticed, (3) surprised, and (4) down-hearted.

A high level of (1) Anger, (2) Sensuality, (3) Fear, and (4) Sadness could be (1) fierce, (2) lascivious, (3) terrified, and (4) anguished.

Mixed emotions are combinations of two or more basic emotions. In the list that follows they are found grouped under the more dominant basic emotion.

19. Susana Bloch, Pedro Orthous, and Guy Sanibanez-H, "Effector Patterns of Basic Emotions: A Psychophysiological Method for Training Actors," Journal of Social Biological Structure, (1987). The words for titling and describing the basic emotions have had a number of name changes by Dr. Bloch. The TEAM uses emotional behavior words referenced in the 1987 article.

[Examples]

Words that imply mixes of two or more basics are (1) greedy, (2) gracious, and (3) mischievous. They are grouped with their dominant basic emotion, (1) greedy: **Anger**/Sadness/Fear, (2) gracious: **Tenderness**/Sadness, (3) mischievous: **Happiness**/Anger/Fear.

The theory behind basic emotions is often compared to color mixing in paints, where there are three primary colors of red, blue, and yellow, and all other colors are either degrees of these primaries achieved by adding white or black, or mixes. Most people can instinctively identify the stronger color in a mix of colors, like recognizing the primary of red in burgundy, magenta, and pink. Some could also identify which of these colors are created by simply adding white to red, as with degrees of pink, or those that are created by mixing in certain degrees of one or more primaries, like mixing blue with red to make purple. The same concept is true of emotionally colored words.

At this point, you don't need to be concerned with which words denote emotions that are either levels of a primary emotion, or mixes of two or more primaries. For purposes of using these words as a method for immediate application to acting, simply understand that if you see a word in a category that doesn't feel to you as if it is an angry word or sensually charged word, that word is most likely listed there to identify the more dominant emotion comprising a complicated mix.

Emotion Words

The list that follows is a rich collection of emotional words that represent states of being, or feelings. As you practice applying these to your acting, you might discover more words to add to each category, compiling your own personal emotion vocabulary.

Think of the words in this list completing either phrase, "to be___" or "to behave with___" by filling in one of the emotion words in the list. For example, "to be outraged" or "to behave with contempt."

Emotions

The numbers and letters (1A, 1B, 2A, 2B, 3A, 3B.) referenced by the emotion indicate the alignment with Postural Attitudes, discussed in the Actions Chapter.

TENDERNESS (1A)

Adoring	Doting	Narcissistic
Affectionate	Dreamy	Mellow
Amiable	Empathetic	Patriotic
Appreciative	Favoring	Pity
Approving	Fondness	Relieved
Benevolent	Friendly	Romantic
Calm	Genial	Satisfied
Caring	Good-hearted	Sensitive
Compassionate	Gracious	Sentimental
Concerned	Gratified	Serene
Considerate	Heartfelt	Sincere
Content	Hospitable	Sympathetic
Cool	Kind	Warm
Cordial	Loving	Warm-hearted
Devoted	Loyal	

ANGER (1B)

Abhorrence	Cantankerous	Ferocious
Acerbic	Chivalrous	Fervent
Adamant	Conceited	Feverish
Aggravated	Confident	Fierce
Aggressive	Contempt	Frustrated
Ambitious	Courageous	Fuming
Annoyed	Cruel	Furious
Arrogant	Curious	Greedy
Assured	Daring	Grumpy
Belligerent	Demanding	Hateful
Bitter	Disdain	Haughty
Bold	Exasperated	Heartless
Brave	Envious	Hostile
Brazen	Fanatical	Indignant

ANGER (1B) *continued*

Impatient	Pompous	Seething
Inquisitive	Predatory	Sour
Insistent	Pretentious	Spiteful
Irate	Proud	Stubborn
Irritated	Raging	Vain
Jealous	Relentless	Valiant
Livid	Resentful	Vehement
Loathsome	Rigid	Vengeful
Malevolent	Ruthless	Vexed
Malicious	Sarcastic	Vicious
Outraged	Sardonic	Willful
Peevish	Savage	Wrathful

SENSUALITY (2A)

Admiration	Enticed	Nonchalant
Amorous	Entranced	Nostalgic
Aroused	Fascinated	Obsessive
Bewitched	Flirtatious	Passive
Breathless	Infatuated	Passionate
Captivated	Inspired	Seductive
Casual	Invigorated	Sensual
Coquettish	Lascivious	Sexual
Coy	Lewd	Voracious
Enamored	Lustful	Wanton
Enraptured	Mesmerized	Wicked
Enthralled		

FEAR (2B)

Aghast	Doubtful	Panicked
Alarmed	Dread	Reluctant
Aloof	Dumbfounded	Repulsed
Amazed	Edgy	Reserved
Anxious	Fidgety	Restless
Appalled	Flabbergasted	Revolted
Apprehensive	Flustered	Sheepish
Astonished	Frantic	Shocked
Astounded	Frazzled	Shy
Baffled	Frenetic	Skeptical
Bashful	Frigid	Spooked
Bewildered	Hesitant	Squeamish
Confounded	Horrified	Stressed
Confused	Hysterical	Stunned
Cowardly	Insecure	Submissive
Crazed	Insulted	Surprised
Dazzled	Intimidated	Suspicious
Demure	Jumpy	Tense
Deranged	Loathsome	Terrified
Disbelief	Meek	Timid
Disapproving	Modest	Uncertain
Disgust	Nauseated	Uneasy
Distrusting	Nervous	Wary
Distracted	Numb	Wild
Distraught	Offended	Worried
Docile	Overwrought	

HAPPINESS (3A)

Amused	Confident	Effervescent
Blissful	Delighted	Elated
Boisterous	Delirious	Enthusiastic
Buoyant	Devilish	Euphoric
Charmed	Eager	Excited
Cheerful	Ecstatic	Exhilarated

HAPPINESS (3A) *continued*

Festive	Jubilant	Rapturous
Frivolous	Lighthearted	Rejoicing
Gay	Merry	Reveling
Grateful	Mirthful	Sly
Happy	Mischievous	Spirited
Intoxicated	Optimistic	Thankful
Jolly	Playful	Vivacious
Jovial		

SADNESS (3B)

Anguished	Embarrassed	Overwhelmed
Apathetic	Forlorn	Pensive
Ashamed	Fretful	Pessimistic
Brooding	Gloomy	Powerless
Cheerless	Glum	Regretful
Crushed	Grave	Remorseful
Defeated	Guilty	Shameful
Dejected	Heartsick	Solemn
Depressed	Heavyhearted	Somber
Desolate	Helpless	Subdued
Despair	Hopeless	Sullen
Desperate	Humbled	Sulking
Despondent	Humiliated	Sorrowful
Devastated	Indifferent	Tearful
Discouraged	Inconsolable	Tormented
Disillusioned	Lonely	Tortured
Dismayed	Lovelorn	Uneasy
Disappointed	Melancholy	Weary
Doleful	Morose	Wistful
Downcast	Mortified	Woeful
Downhearted	Mournful	Yearn

Emotional Embodiment

As stated earlier, recognizing and expressing mixed emotions are highly subjective acts. An individual's environment, culture, and physiological make-up influence how that person expresses the varying degrees of mixed emotions. However, the basic emotions are common to all, and a technique like Alba Emoting can help you understand how to manifest and modulate the basic emotions, as well as develop more accurate recognition of the individual elements in mixed emotions. Until you have the opportunity to study such a technique, practicing the interpretation and embodiment of emotions will help you prepare for the lessons that follow. Below are some suggestions for such practice.

Exercise
Exploring Emotional Embodiment

A	B	C
1. Irritated	Proud	Outraged
2. Loving	Sympathetic	Gratified
3. Sensual	Fascinated	Voracious
4. Nervous	Distrusting	Horrified
5. Amused	Optimistic	Exhilarated
6. Sullen	Embarrassed	Despondent

PART I: Using the emotion words provided above, stand in front of a full length mirror with closed eyes and "take on the emotion" by imagining yourself in that state of being, and allowing your body posture, facial expression, and even your breath adjust into your interpretation of the emotion. Then open your eyes, and see your interpretation of that emotion in the mirror.

Keep practicing this process with the words across the page, from column A to C, and down the list. What subtle differences emerge, and where, as you adjust your expressive state to match the word?

PART II: Working with a partner, stand a few paces away from each other, and with backs facing each other. Using the emotion words provided at the beginning of this exercise, each of you close your eyes and "take on the emotion," as referenced earlier. Turn and share your interpretation of the same emotion word with your partner.

Do you both look the same? If not, what are the differences and why? Talk about any subtle differences in interpretation and expression of the emotion word you just explored. Keep practicing this process with the words across the page, from column A to C, and down the list.

PART III: Working with a partner, stand a few paces away from each other, and with backs facing each other. Using the emotion words provided at the beginning of this exercise, each of you close your eyes and "take on the emotion," as referenced earlier. Turn and share your interpretation of the same emotion word with your partner, while saying the line, "What are you looking at?" Do you both sound the same? If not, what are the differences and why? Talk about any subtle differences in line delivery as well as any additional gestures and movement that occurred due to the act of speaking. Below are a few more lines to apply as you continue this exercise through the rest of the word list.

What did you say?

I heard you.

No, thank you.

Good morning.

Where are you going?

Would you like to come along?

I just need some time alone.

PART IV: Working with a partner, stand a few paces away from each other, facing each other. Using the emotion words provided at the beginning of this exercise, one partner "takes on the emotion," as referenced earlier, while the other partner watches. The partner who shares the emotive word interpretation does so using any one of the dialogue lines listed previously. The partner who observed now adopts the expressive embodiment and vocal qualities of the other, and delivers back the same line, gestures, and posture, acting like a mirror for the original presenter.

If the observing partner did not know in advance which emotion word was being explored, was the partner able to guess the word after it was demonstrated? When the observer acts as the mirror, is an accurate match accomplished? If not, what are the differences and why? What is it like to embody someone else's interpretation of an emotion? Keep practicing this process with the words across the page, from column A to C, and down the list. Invite a third person to watch the exchange and point out any differences that are not first observed by those embodying the emotions.

Note: Continued practice of Parts I-IV with new emotion words from the lists provided in this chapter, or additional words you would like to explore, is encouraged.

Try This:

Watch the beginning scene of a movie with the sound turned off. While tracking the body language and facial expressions of a character, see if you can score her/his Emotional Colors using the words from the lists provided previously. Then, watch the scene again with the sound turned back on and see whether listening to the sound of the voice and hearing the words either changes your choices or confirms them. Can you tell when the actor is using conscious Emotion Tactics and when the actor is reacting to the given circumstances with Emotional Colors? If so, how can you tell?

Mother and Daughter Scene

Two young student actors in my acting class are working on the mother/daughter scene in Wendy Wasserstein's play Third. *The students have prepared Emotion Tactics for the scene and as I watch them run an in-class rehearsal, the scene comes off as a disagreement based solely in anger. Their scene has very little give-and-take with this purely argumentative approach. There are few moments of discoveries and very little dramatic arc to the scene. It comes across as one big angry fight, with very few Emotional Colors and not a lot of information about the characters' relationship or what is at stake in the scene. I ask to see their score of Emotion Tactics, and I notice that most of their tactics are chosen from words under the general category of Anger.*

We sit and have a short discussion about all the possible ways in which people can have disagreements over subjects. We also talk about a technique for consciously choosing opposites, or less obvious Emotion Tactics, which can create much more interesting and dynamic interactions in a scene. I encourage the actors to score their scene again, purposely looking for different ways to handle their conflicting viewpoints—such as, at times they could be doubtful, amused, or uneasy, instead of being outraged.

The two actors then pore through the lists of Emotion Tactics and engage in discussion of their options. Soon they are on their feet and rehearsing the scene again. When I stop by to see how the scene is coming along— the scene is absolutely riveting. The actors have found so many new levels to this mother/daughter relationship simply by rescoring the Emotion Tactics. Now there seems to be so much more at stake in this disagreement. Their relationship now appears to have a sense of history, as one character finds something funny or ironic in what the other says—as if it had been said many times before. In another moment they make loving choices of tenderness and care, showing a glimpse that one hopes to end this disagreement and make amends. The student actors recognize the change as well, and find that they even enjoy acting the scene so much more. They are far more in tune with each other throughout the scene and care more about the outcome.

Building Character Personality and the Social Mask

Selecting Emotional Colors is an excellent basis for building a character's personality and source of behavior. When we first attempt to describe a person, in order to share the sense of who that person is, we might initially offer a, "This is what he looks like" descriptor. But then we often launch into emotional descriptions of their states of being: "He's...goofy, a serious type, intense, a little scattered at times, a riot, very friendly, a loose cannon, or sweet." When approaching the study of a character, it is a good practice to create a list of emotion words that describe how your character behaves and what you believe are the building blocks of the character's personality.

It is also important to recognize that we tend to have a public persona, much like wearing a mask. We might adopt this social facade when around people we don't know very well. This social mask can project how we want to be perceived by others or can serve as a protective shield against those we don't yet trust. As you prepare a role, think about possible social masks and how they may differ depending on who your character is with, and where and when they may prefer to adopt a facade.

When the mask is dropped, even for brief moments, it reveals greater truths about what we are really thinking. These moments can be prolonged periods of time when we are amongst those that we know better or trust, or they can be quick flashes of gut reactions when we are caught off guard, and respond honestly. What are some possible candid reactions for your character, and what might those moments reveal?

When constructing a character's personality and the behavior associated with these choices, Emotion Tactics and Colors are essential building blocks for character development.

Exercise for Emotional Layers in Character

After examining your character's story throughout the script, see if you can identify the following:

1. A primary basic emotion (Anger, Tenderness, Fear, Sensuality, Sadness, or Happiness) that is a dominant through-line for your character's

behavior during the entire story. This would reflect your character's core, revealed when with trusted acquaintances and when not feeling threatened by others.

2. A secondary basic emotion that is your character's social mask. This is what your character prefers to exhibit in public, to those unfamiliar, and is the preferred persona for formal settings.

3. A third basic emotion that might be your character's shadow self. This is the rare emotion that rises up quickly, unannounced and uncontrollable, perhaps when your character feels threatened, tired, or insecure.

After identifying these three basic emotions and understanding how and when they would be used, you can (1) use them for an overall embodiment guide for your character and (2) use them now as a guide for selecting Emotion Tactics when scoring your scene.

In order to apply these emotion layers to character embodiment, go to the Actions chapter section on Postural Attitudes. You can practice embodying each basic emotion chosen in this exercise and find a blend of the three Postural Attitudes for your character's overall expressive behavior.

The following exercise will guide you through the process of selecting Emotion Tactics and scoring a scene. When assigning Emotion Tactics to a scene, choose ones that are grouped in the categories of the basic emotions you identified for your character's primary, facade, and shadow states. This keeps your tactic choices in line with the script research and personality preparations you made for your character.

Exercise
Applying Emotion Tactics to Open Scenes

Open scenes are created for actors to exercise their acting choices. They do not have identified characters and are written in such a way that the scenes can happen anywhere, anytime, with any combination of situations, given circumstances, and objectives. For purposes of exercising your ability to connect Emotion Tactics to text, say each of the lines in the open scene that follows with the different emotions listed for each line. With the four columns of Emotion

Tactics provided, you have four different possible readings of the open scene.

The Basic Exercise:

With a scene partner read the scene out loud, applying the Emotion Tactics from column #1. Then read the scene again with tactics in #2, #3, and #4. Notice how the intensity of the scene changes as you move across the columns of Emotion Tactics. Does one set of tactics seem to raise the scene's intensity more than any other?

To explore this exercise in greater depth, follow these instructions:

1. Stand and face your partner.

2. Each of you secretly select a column of Emotion Tactics. In order to find the tactic quickly and easily, fold the page so your Emotion Tactic column rests just to the right of the dialogue.

3. Apply this basic rule to the scene: When your partner is delivering a line to you, maintain eye contact with your scene partner and react instinctively.

4. Progress through the scene slowly, allowing a pause after each line delivery to listen and react to what was said and how it was said to you. REACT instinctively. Then, look down at your score for your Emotion Tactic and the next line.

5. Deliver the next line applying your tactic, which might be considerably different than your instinctive reaction. Continue through the entire scene in this way, discovering instinctive reactions and practicing conscious emotional actions applied to text.

Keep in mind that this is an exercise that provides plenty of practice with large emotional swings from line to line. It would be highly unusual to have a scene where there is a different Emotion Tactic for every single line.

OPEN SCENE

Dialogue	Emotion Tactics			
	#1	#2	#3	#4
A: Hi.	Lustful	Depressed	Alarmed	Bitter
B: Hello.	Annoyed	Considerate	Aroused	Festive
A: Great outfit.	Dazzled	Sarcastic	Bashful	Baffled
B: Thanks.	Coy	Aloof	Fascinated	Confused
A: Where did you get it?	Envious	Cool	Gracious	Insistent
B: It's my own.	Playful	Doubtful	Coquettish	Adamant
A: Your own?	Shocked	Amused	Disbelieving	Playful
B: Yes. Mine.	Curious	Despondent	Peevish	Obsessive
A: Wow!	Downcast	Haughty	Delighted	Raging
B: Thanks.	Cheerless	Detesting	Apprehensive	Distraught
A: I mean it.	Nervous	Sly	Benevolent	Vexed
B: Well – again, thanks.	Embarrassed	Aggravated	Lighthearted	Cowardly

Dialogue	Emotion Tactics			
	#1	#2	#3	#4
A: So? I was wondering…	Affectionate	Buoyant	Excited	Insistent
B: Wondering?	Apprehensive	Irritated	Fervent	Distrusting
A: If you could…	Doting	Amused	Aggressive	Flirtatious
B: Really?	Uneasy	Impatient	Invigorated	Thankful
A: Do you mind?	Appreciative	Astounded	Fervent	Gracious
B: No.	Mortified	Disgusted	Lascivious	Charmed
A: No? …. Or No?	Bewildered	Wicked	Anxious	Lonely
B: No.	Rigid	Delirious	Breathless	Fond
A: All right then.	Forlorn	Ferocious	Entranced	Affectionate
B: Ok.	Disdainful	Hateful	Confident	Enraptured

After reading the four variations of the open scene, discuss what was different with each reading when you changed the Emotion Tactic for each line.

1. What did you discover when you gave yourself time to instinctively react before selecting an Emotion Tactic? Can you see how at a faster pace this could translate into a scene filled with flashes of honest, emotional reactions and then consciously applied Emotion Tactics?

2. Without even planning a scenario or given circumstances, did a character relationship seem to appear simply by applying these Emotion Tactics?

Revisit the open scene, applying one column of tactics. Practice the scene very slowly at first, finding candid reactions, and then applying Emotion Tactics. During additional runs of the scene, gradually speed up the interaction process, allowing the reaction time to shorten and faster delivery of the returning line and Emotion Tactic. Eventually, run the scene, in "real time" and see how the reactions, or Emotional Colors, become minute flashes, and the Emotion Tactics merge into instinctive application with text. With this practice, you will start to see how this technique can reveal a dynamic scene with layers of feelings, reactions, and interactions. Emotional variations can provide relationship subtext, evidence of character motivation, and greater depth of a story unfolding through dialogue. The combinations are infinite, and so then is your acting range!

Stories Emerge from Emotional Scores

I hand the Applying Emotion Tactics to Text exercise to my Acting II class, and break them into teams of two. One actor plays character A, and one plays B. Each actor is to select a column of Emotion Tactics and apply them to the open scene. They are instructed to keep playing the scene over and over again, following these basic instructions:

Take your time; be sure to watch the delivery of the actor across from you; notice how you want to react impulsively. REACT. This will be the emotionally colored, honest reaction to what you are receiving from your scene partner. Then look down on the paper, pick up your Emotion Tactic and line, and play the line with the Emotion Tactic in response. This will help you see how your character could also choose a controlled, conscious Emotion Tactic, or cover up the previous honest reaction. Progress through the scene in this manner, and take your time.

The teams spread out around the acting space and apply this exercise. They make discoveries as they find their way through these Emotion Tactics and Colors. The room buzzes with excitement as exhilarated and varied levels of emotions emerge in this open, content-less scene. Actual scenes emerge with dynamic interactions, intense relationships, keen observations, truthful reactions, and strong, tactical maneuvers. After a while I stop the exercise and ask, "So—even though this is a scene without an obvious story, did anyone find that stories and individual objectives emerged?" Most of the students' hands shoot up and we engage in an exciting dialogue of shared discoveries. The students recognize that by applying Emotional Colors and tactics to this content-less scene, content and meaning quickly emerge.

Try This:

Working with a partner, take a set of index cards and write one line of text on each index card. These lines can be pulled randomly from any script, or they can be simple common sayings. To start, your partner selects a random Emotion Tactic for you from the lists provided in this chapter. Shuffle the index cards up and pick one at random. Say the line on the index card to your partner while applying the Emotion Tactic. Discard that index card and switch roles, with you selecting the emotion and your partner now selecting a new line from the shuffled index cards. Keep going back and forth until you have performed all the lines on the index cards. Does any kind of meaning or scene emerge from this random selection of lines and emotions? Do you find your thoughts automatically searching for meanings, attempting to connect the dots between these random emotional statements? If so, you are constructing a story through your own human need to create a whole from individual parts.

Breaking a Scene into Beats

Tactics are used for a certain period of time, and when the tactic is not producing desired results, we naturally shift to a new choice. In acting, this shift is the act of moving into a new beat. It is important to recognize beats within a script so you know where to apply these varying tactics.

In the Thoughts chapter we discussed the objectives that lead the character in a specific direction. Once headed in that direction, the actor must understand how to navigate the twists and turns in the character's journey. This navigation process is where tactics are applied.

How difficult would it be to read a book that was written like one long continuous paragraph, failing to identify shifts in subject matter? Paragraphs in writing identify shifting points and signpost changes within a larger body of work; likewise, changes in tactics project the shifting points in the performance of a scene. The conscious shifting points in acting are called beats.

Beat shifts are motivated by the character's thoughts, emotions, and actions. We will address them now in this chapter to help you understand how these beat shifts will affect your Emotion Tactics and then later, in the Actions Chapter, your Action Tactics. Keep in mind that emotions are present in our thoughts and actions. So when we later refer to a change of action or a change of subject, remember that emotions and feelings are present in these activities.

Beats

A script can be broken down into scenes, and those scenes can be broken into beats. A beat is the smallest unit in a script in which a beginning, middle, and end to a subject or action are implied. Some acting techniques use Beat Objectives to title their beats, reminding the actor that this is indeed a unit of action that requires an objective or desired outcome. Other acting techniques title a beat with tactics and use verbs to identify the action of that beat. The TEAM uses Emotion Tactics and Action Tactics to title beats. This reminds the actor that emotions and physical actions create expressive behavior that contribute to the overall success, or victory of the objective.

Using either approach of "beating a script" with behavioral choices is often called scoring, for it resembles the process of breaking down music into measures. However, a beat in a theatrical script cannot be measured by beats per minute or measure, like in music. The beats in a script are measured by identifying minor changes in subject matter or behavior.

A new beat is signified by one of the following:

1. Your character's introduction of a new subject

2. Your character's attempt at a new Emotion Tactic

3. Your character's attempt at a new Action Tactic

Character Perspective Initiates Beat Shifts

When an actor breaks a scene into beats, it is always from the perspective of her own character. A beat shift occurs when your character must deal with new subject matter, introduced by herself or someone else, or when she initiates a new Action Tactic or Emotion Tactic. If she shifts to the new topic or tactic, it is a new beat. If someone else shifts to a new subject, but your character still acts upon her original topic—ignoring or overriding the other subject introduced—she maintains the same beat.

[**Example**] Think about a time in your life when you were having a conversation with someone and you were intent upon discussing a specific topic. During this conversation the other person may have interrupted and initiated a new subject. At the time you were faced with two choices: (1) finishing your thought and continuing with your subject, or (2) temporarily going along with the change of subject proposed by the other. You might have continued the conversation while also looking for the opportunity to swing it back to your agenda.

Keep in mind, your character IS the protagonist of her story, and the driving force of her journey. So all beat shifts occur for your character, and by your character's own will.

[**Example**] Imagine your character is a business person caught up in persuading a client to go out on a date rather than attending to the client's need to make a business deal. Your character flatters the client and tries to keep the subject on their social lives. Meanwhile, the client interjects, trying to keep the conversation on business. Your character ignores these interjections, remaining dedicated to the dating objective and tactic of flattery.

In this example, your character's beat would not change, though the actor playing the client could have several beat changes, trying to bring the conversation back to solidifying a deal. However, consider the same situation and same subject matter in the scene but have your character try a new Emotion Tactic:

[**Example**] Your character is a business person caught up in persuading a client to go out on a date rather than attending to the client's need to make a business deal. Your character flatters the client and tries to keep the subject on their social lives. Meanwhile, the client interjects, trying to keep the subject on business. Your character then ridicules the client, implying that the client is no fun and too serious while still focusing on talk of their social lives. Your character uses this new tactic, realizing that casual flirting is not working.

Here the subject did not change, but your character tried a new tactic—*to ridicule* rather than *to flatter*—to accomplish the objective. The subject remained the same, talking about their social lives. There are two beats in this example because your character is using a new tactic.

Try This:

Scripts are made up primarily of dialogue, essentially a conversation between two or more people. Our day-to-day conversations with others have noticeable beats as well, particularly if they are led by strong intentions or objectives. Reflect on a good conversation you had recently. What made it a good conversation? Try tracking through the conversation, not word-by-word but subject-by-subject. As you do this, see if you can recall who shifted the subjects and how they shifted. By doing this you have just completed the first level of a Beat Score for your conversation. Shifting in and out of beats in conversation is common human behavior. Subconsciously, you were probably aware of it the entire time, but now you have approached it consciously, the way an actor must when scoring a script.

Emotion Coaching for a Large Cast

I am the Emoting Coach for 75 actors in a community theatre project directed by nationally recognized community performance director, Dr. Richard Geer. Richard and I are both practitioners of the Alba Emoting technique for embodying emotion. He has asked me to work with his acting company to help them connect with the Emotional Colors and tactics in this dynamic performance piece.

Most of the performers in this play, ranging in ages from four to 80, have never acted before. They are not practiced in scoring a script for emotions, nor are they familiar with how to embody those choices in their performance. This will be the first time I have explored methods for coaching emotional embodiment techniques to such a large group of performers in a very short amount of time.

My responsibility is to attend the table talk for each scene and develop a quick plan for assisting the actors with embodiment. I listen to their scene read-throughs and discussions—while I quietly score the scenes with basic emotions. At the end of each discussion, Richard asks me to share my scoring discoveries. Once we feel these are in line with the director's vision, I engage the actors in a few exercises in core embodiment techniques for the emotions identified.

Richard also double casts all the roles in his projects with Cast A and Cast B designations. This way all the community members engaged in this performance project can still attend to their life responsibilities when needed, knowing their double can stand in for them. Working with the doubles in each scene proved to be a delightful reminder of the dualistic nature of emotional embodiment. Each actor brings their life-learned emotional patterns to playing the character as well as their interpretation of the situation being played. Even though the basic emotions scored in each scene were the same from one scene to the next, each double played the scene with their own unique embodiments and interpretations springing from individual personalities.

I found myself attending final performances many times, as did other audience members, eager to see how cast A members may play a scene differently than cast B members. An exciting observation, indeed!

When examining beat shifts in a script, remember that each are mini objectives or tactics building toward the Scene Objective. The Scene Objectives all contribute as building blocks to the Main Objective, and the Main Objective steers us in the far future toward the character's Super Objective. Think about how a manufacturing company may use an assembly line process, where each section of the factory only produces one part of the final product. All areas on the assembly line have the ultimate intention to produce the same item, and yet each piece of the production process has its own specific and immediate need and design. When acting a role, every choice you make as the character is intended as an action for gaining ground toward a larger objective.

Beat Shifts and Obstacles

It may appear at times that character behaviors are not obviously leading toward the next objective. In this case you must ask yourself if your character is presently met with an obstacle.

[**Example**] The business person, mentioned previously, wants to ask the client out on a date and uses flattery as an emotional tactic. The client is very defensive, which is an obstacle. The business person changes the tactic to ridicule, attempting to overcome this obstacle by disarming the client's defensiveness with a very different tactic.

The choice of ridicule may appear as if it is not serving the objective, *to get my client to go on a date with me.* This new tactic is dealing directly with the obstacle presented by the client, *defensiveness. Ridiculing* is an attempt to disarm *defensiveness.* A follow-up tactical choice after disarming could be, *to be aloof.* This may motivate the client to reconnect with the business person again in order to gain acceptance. After all, the client still has the intention of closing a deal. By using aloofness, the business person may regain control of the scene and then be able to return to the primary Scene Objective.

Any obstacles met in the scene must be overcome, using various emotion or Action Tactics, until the character is successful. Any change your character makes as an attempt to overcome these obstacles involves a beat shift. The actor's job here is to make sense of the logic used by the character overcoming these obstacles.

Exercise
Identifying Beats in an Open Scene

Below is the same open scene you explored earlier in this chapter. Read the scene, applying the following:

(1) Create a Scene Objective for A: _____

(2) See if you can identify the beat shifts for character A.

A: Hi.

B: Hello.

A: Great outfit.

B: Thanks.

A: Where did you get it?

B: It's my own.

A: Your own?

B: Yes. Mine.

A: Wow!

B: Thanks.

A: I mean it.

B: Well – again, thanks.

A: So? I was wondering...

B: Wondering?

A: If you could...

B: Really?

A: Do you mind?

B: No.

A: No? .... Or No?

B: No.

A: All right then.

B: Ok.

Objectives Influence Beat Shifts

Depending on the objective you choose for A, the scene could vary greatly in its flow, delivery, and beat breakdown.

[**Example**] If you choose for A the objective, *to get him to give me back the jacket he stole*, and if A's first Emotion Tactic is insistently applied, then the lines between "Hi" through "Your own?" could all be one beat. That's because the meanings within the lines in this section can support an insistent Emotion Tactic—*to address the jacket.*

If the objective for A is *to ask B out on a date*, the first beat could apply a casual Emotion Tactic—*to acknowledge contact* with "Hi" and "Hello." Then, the tactic for the next beat could be *to admire*, as A compliments B on the outfit.

Do you think the beat shifts in the scene would be different if (1) A's objective was *to get B's autograph* (B is a famous clothing designer) or (2) if A's objective was *to get B to lend me his jacket* (so A can enter a formal, jacket-required restaurant)? Try applying these two objectives to the scene, and see how the beats could shift around, depending on the objective of the character.

Perspective Motivates Tactics

A perspective, or an individual's way of regarding situations and judging their relative importance, can also influence how a score sheet varies from one person to the other. The actor is determining the character's perspective on the situation. In his book, *Building a Character*, Stanislavski reminds actors that perspective is conveyed through thoughts, feelings, and vivid illustration, or action.[20]

[**Example**] In the open scene the A-character can't enter a jacket-required restaurant unless he borrows the jacket off of the back of the B-character, who is coming out of the restaurant. One actor may decide that the perspective of the A-character is urgent, stressed, and always seeing the "glass half full." Another actor playing the same role may believe that his character is casual, playful, and optimistic.

These choices in the character's perspective will greatly vary the thoughts, feelings, and actions conveyed in the same situation. In this example, the characters' Emotion Tactics would certainly influence the delivery of lines and actions, making these two interpretations of the same scene quite different.

More details about how to use Emotion Tactics are offered later in this chapter, and the Actions chapter explains how to use Action Tactics in the beats. For now, understand that your beat identification and choice of tactics will vary from someone else's and that personal perspective guides the beat shift and the tactics in the beat. With this in mind, it is important to articulate the reason for the beat shift.

20. Constantine Stanislavski, *Building a Character* (New York: Routledge, 1977), 173.

Beat Subtext

Beat Subtext scoring is applying a short personal message to the beginning of a beat, which expresses the character's perspective on the beat shift. It is written in the language of the character's honest thoughts, as if the character is talking to himself about what he is really thinking and discovering in the moment. The Beat Subtext provides you with a clear connection to the character's true feelings about, and reasoning for, this shift. It is a form of mini-inner-monologue, or what Stanislavski referred to as utilizing your "inner motive forces."[21] It is essentially what the character is thinking as he reacts and interacts with others. It is the secret inner voice of reasoning, desire, motivation, and contemplation. It is what is not said but instead is felt and reflected in the character's behavior.

[**Example**] Let's look at the open scene example of the famous person and the autograph situation, where A wants to get B's autograph. Below are some examples of possible Beat Subtext Statements that would guide the actor through her beat shifts.

Lines	Beat Subtext
A: Hi.	"Oh! Is it really you?!"
B: Hello.	
A: Great outfit.	"Quick, find something to talk about—the jacket."
B: Thanks.	
A: Where did you get it?	
B: It's my own.	
A: Your own?	
B: Yes. Mine.	

21. Stanislavski, *An Actor Prepares*, 244.

A: Wow!   "I thought I knew everything about you, but...you do clothing design too!"

B: Thanks.

A: I mean it.

B: Well – again, thanks.

A: So? I was wondering...   "Don't let her get away without at least asking!"

B: Wondering?

A: If you could...

The Beat Subtext should be a short phrase or sentence that captures the character's private thoughts as she shifts focus for the coming beat. This Subtext Statement identifies the reasoning for the beat shift while also revealing your character's feelings about this shift. The Subtext Statement will then provide a pathway to (1) steer you in the direction of Emotion Tactics and Actions and (2) help you make Personal Connections with your character's tactics and beat shifts.

[**Example**] Beat Subtext occurs all the time, in real life. How often are you in conversation with someone while running your own commentary in your head? During this conversation you might be dwelling on the subject you really want to bring up with the person while engaging in small talk. You might be fixated on something you are honestly trying to get out of the person, but you can't quite come right out and say what you honestly want.

If you realize that this internal monologue could just as easily be going on with your character as well, the Beat Subtext will start to make complete sense as you use it to motivate beat shifts as well as actions and reactions within the scene.

Beat Subtexts Help Actor with Simple Dialogue

I am directing Tennessee Williams' This Property is Condemned. The play depicts two teenagers meeting on a section of railroad track. The young man, Tom, has skipped school to fly his kite but encounters a peculiar girl whom he has heard stories about from friends at school. The actor playing Tom is feeling very challenged by his character's extremely simple lines, which are reactions to the girl's many stories of her life and to her explanations for why she is now living in a condemned house. Without clear, strong choices made by the actor playing Tom, this play could easily portray this character as simply a passive listener to this talkative girl.

Tom's lines are often very short comments like, "Oh," "uh-huh," "Yeah?" "Naw?" or "What?" As a matter of fact, in this short 10–minute play, Tom says, "Naw" and "What?" six times each and "Yeah" eleven times. The rest of his lines are mostly short questions like, "Who was...?" or "How do you...? or "What happened...?" The few times Tom actually expresses an opinion or personal wish, provide us with important clues to what he really wants in the scene. Actually, the character of Tom provides one of those rare occasions in scripts where the character clearly states his objective, perhaps due to his young age and his capability of speaking his truth. Tom comes right out and states that he heard that she took his friend Frank inside the condemned house and danced for him with her clothes off. Tom proceeds to ask if she would now do that for him. The actor playing Tom decides that Tom's Scene Objective is to get her to agree to dance naked for him.

The actor decides to use Subtext Statements as a way to connect with these rather banal lines. He goes through the text and meticulously writes out his true thoughts for each of these lines, particularly the lines that cause him to react and shift the action whenever possible. Soon his "Yeah" and "Naw" lines are motivated by subtext thoughts like, "Well, you just busted my bubble!," "I can't walk these stupid train tracks as well as you!," "I feel bad for her," and "If the house is empty, we can get-it-on in there." The many questioning lines about people and events in her stories now have greater motivation as well: "Who cares about the railroad men! Aren't you interested in me?", "Alright, enough about Alva already!" and "I never heard of that. Is it something kinky?"

We then ask a fellow actor from another play in our Tennessee Williams play festival to call out these Subtext Statements during a rehearsal of the scene. At first it is a funny process to hear the true thoughts of this young character pursuing his sexual desires; however, once we accept hearing these truths called out by an actor on the side-lines, we soon start to enjoy how the actor playing Tom immediately embodies the emotions and behaviors connected to these thoughts. After going through the scene twice using this method, he starts to automatically imbue the simple lines with layers of meaning, feeling, and reaction. The scene eventually becomes a charming exchange between the two characters, and the actor no longer struggles with the simplistic lines.

Exercise
Attaching Emotions to Beat Shift Subtext

Practice applying Subtext Statements, for character A by following these steps:

1. Read the scene aloud, including reading the Subtext Statements out loud.

2. See if you can allow the Subtext Statement to influence your delivery of the lines and your behavior as character A.

3. Notice how your partner, character B responds to this delivery.

4. Then, read the scene with the subtext as a silent thought in your mind, but which influences your behavior.

5. After examining your feelings and behavior while using these Subtext Statements, can you identify different Emotion Tactics that represent these feelings and actions? Do they match with the ones listed in the far right column, or do you identify with other Emotion Tactics?

6. Try applying the Emotion Tactics listed in the far right column. Read the scene once by delivering your lines starting with choice #1, and then read the scene again applying choice #2 in the Emotion Tactic column. If you discovered other emotion words in step #5, read the scene applying these to each beat.

After exercising the open scene with these six steps, can you recognize how the delivery of the scene changes? How does character B's reactions change your own delivery? Can you identify the Scene Objective for character A by using the Subtext Statements as a guide?

Lines	Subtext Statement for Character A	Emotion Tactics for A
A: Hi.	"I haven't seen you in a while!"	(1) Festive
B: Hello.		(2) Downcast
A: Great outfit.	"That jacket would fit me perfectly"	(1) Envious
B: Thanks.		(2) Sly
A: Where did you get it?	"Is this a rental?"	(1) Insistent
B: It's my own.		(2) Flirtatious
A: Your own?	"Perfect for lending to me!"	(1) Playful
B: Yes. Mine.		(2) Fondly
A: Wow!		
B: Thanks.		
A: I mean it.		
B: Well – again, thanks.		

Emotions

A: So? I was wondering…	"Let's get this awkward request over with"	(1) Nervous
B: Wondering?		(2) Amused
A: If you could…		

B: Really?	"Don't make me beg in front of my date!"	(1) Fervent
A: Do you mind?		(2) Buoyant

B: No.	"You don't really mean – No."	(1) Affectionate
A: No? …. Or No?		(2) Bewildered

B: No.	"What a selfish bastard!"	(1) Disdainful
A: All right then.		(2) Depressed
B: Ok.		

Exercise
Beat Subtext Reveals Personality

Earlier in this chapter we talked about building character embodiment by considering three possible layers:

1. A primary, basic emotion that is a dominant through-line for your character's behavior during the entire story. This would reflect your character's core, revealed when with trusted acquaintances and when not feeling threatened by others.
2. A secondary basic emotion that is your character's social mask. This is what your character prefers to exhibit in public, to

those unfamiliar, and is the preferred persona for formal settings.

3. A third basic emotion that might be your character's shadow self. This is the rare emotion that rises up quickly, unannounced and uncontrollable, perhaps when your character feels threatened, tired, or insecure.

Using one of the short scenes provided in **Appendix C**, apply Subtext Statements in the following ways:

1. Use Subtext Statements throughout the scene that remain true to your character's primary emotional through-line. What Emotion Tactics and Emotional Colors are revealed by this perspective?

2. Use Subtext Statements throughout the scene that remain true to your character's secondary emotional facade, or social mask. How does the scene change when your character is wearing a social mask? What Emotion Tactics and Emotional Colors emerge here?

3. Identify a time in the scene where your character might resort to the third emotional layer, or shadow self. What does this reveal about your character and the situation?

4. Try to include all three layers of emotional traits in the scene as you create your Subtext Statements. What is revealed about your character, and the tone of the scene when all three layers are revealed?

5. Prepare the scene with an opposite approach. Start by scoring the scene with Emotion Tactics, and then see what Subtext Statements are revealed. Do you make new discoveries about the scene and the character by working from this direction first?

6. Create a Scene Objective for your character, and work from this direction first. Then break the scene into beats, and assign Subtext Statements to each of the beats based on your character's objective. Are your Subtext Statements exposing your character's primary through-line, social mask, or shadow self? Or do they

naturally vary, depending on the text or actions of your partner playing the opposite character?

Subtext Statement Checklist

☐ Is the subtext written in a short phrase or sentence?

☐ Is the subtext encased in quotes to clarify it is from your character's perspective?

☐ Does the content of the subtext capture the essence of the changing subject, Emotion Tactic, or Action Tactic?

☐ Does the tone of the subtext express strong, honest feelings about the situation?

☐ Is the thought or feeling expressed in the subtext in line with the goals of your character's objective?

Try This:

Pick any scene from a script, select a character to play, and then break the scene into beats. Read the scene out loud to yourself or with a scene partner, and spontaneously speak your subtext as soon as you recognize that your character is shifting a beat, even if you are speaking over the lines of your scene partner. Be as spontaneous as you can blurting out the first thoughts that come to your mind, no matter how strange or raw they may sound at first. Do this many times and with various scenes and characters. With practice you will eventually find that you can instinctively feel where the beats shift, and instead of voicing the subtext, you will find yourself thinking it, reacting to it, and applying it to your behavior.

The Arc of the Scene

The final step in making emotion choices for a scene is recognizing the arc of the scene and how these choices support the arc. The arc is a bend in the scene, or a curve of building tension. The arc of a scene is the moment where tension builds in a scene until it reaches a climactic point, or the place of highest tension, and then subsides.

The arc is much like the tension you might feel increase as you walk up a hill. Imagine that the path gets very steep toward the top and you encounter many large rocks in your way. You persist, laboring up the hill and around the rocks until you find a moment where it evens out and you feel your body momentarily release from the struggle. A scene is often written with this kind of built-in tension, often caused by maneuvering around obstacles.

It is important for an actor to recognize the arc of a scene and reserve the most intense tactics and behaviors for the arc. This supports a build of tension, leading to a climax, and then finishes with a moment of release. Stanislavski called this "restraint and finish."[22] Too often, actors will start a scene making the biggest, most aggressive choices, thinking it will make them look good in their acting. However, they accomplish the opposite. They come into the scene and shoot directly to the top of the arc with great intensity, leaving very little growth for the scene. Stanislavski recommends using restraint in choices early in the scene, so as not to charge right for the arc. He advises the actor to release some of the control exhibited earlier in the scene and finish with greater urgency and intensity as the scene starts to come to a close.

Keep in mind that dynamic acting does not necessarily mean to be big, boisterous, and loud. It can also mean being intriguing, unique, inventive, mysterious, extraordinary, and creative. Save the big stuff for the climax.

One of the greatest influences on the levels of conflict in a scene is the use of Emotion Tactics. As you construct your choices in the scene, select the less aggressive and lower–level Emotion Tactics for the beginning of the scene. Unless the script demands a strong entrance and clearly steers you toward the more intense choices in the beginning, hold back and select more subtle, intriguing choices to help build interest and mystery. Then, allow the beats that lead you toward the climax of the scene to build with more aggressive tactics and

22. Stanislavski, *Building a Character,*79.

extremes in Emotional Colors for the big finish. Finally, allow your character to come back down, even briefly, at the end of the scene to some point of resolve. Unless the script requires you to storm out or burst into tears or peals of laughter, allow your character—and in effect, the audience—to soak in what happened by experiencing a release of tension. The release can simply mean that you have dropped down a level in intensity, and it does not necessarily mean that you are serene, complacent, or subdued. Your acting craft comes in strongly here as you make choices that tell the character's story with many levels, builds, fights, falls, vulnerabilities, and resting points.

Guidelines for Choosing Emotion Tactics

- ❑ Select a singular word that reflects a feeling, emotion, or state of being.

- ❑ Select words that appear to stem from basic emotions.

- ❑ Fully understand the meaning of the word used and how it would affect your character's state of emotional being.

- ❑ Steer clear of words that are too intellectual, which keep you from full embodiment.

- ❑ Keep in mind basic emotions that reflect your character's core personality traits, preferred social mask, and darker shadow self.

- ❑ Use the Subtext Statement to guide your Emotion Tactic choices.

- ❑ Allow as many Emotional Colors and Emotion Tactics in a beat as necessary for actions, reactions, and impulses to occur.

- ❑ Consider the arc of the scene when selecting Emotion Tactics throughout the scene.

- ❑ Consider opposites, or antithetical thinking, when selecting emotion words so you don't select obvious or trite choices.

Exercise
Playing the Arc with Two Different Approaches

In **Appendix C** you will find sample scenes for practice. Either work with that scene or use the grid provided to work with another scene, and follow these instructions for exploring the same scene with two different approaches.

Approach #1: Select a character to portray and approach the scene by identifying Beat Subtext Statements, beat changes, and then Emotion Tactics. Identify the arc of the scene and intentionally place stronger, more intense tactics near the arc to increase conflict and raise urgency. Read the scene out loud, to yourself, or with a partner, applying these choices. Can you identify the character's need, objective, and victory for the scene?

Approach #2: Now use a different approach to scene work. Select the other character to portray, or choose a new scene, and this time identify your character's need, objective, and victory statement. Then read the scene out loud to yourself, or with a partner, applying truth and belief in this need and desired outcome. Are you able to gradually recognize beat shifts, subtext, and Emotion Tactics? Can you identify the arc of the scene and where the strongest Emotion Tactics could be best used?

With both approaches to scene work, do you also notice Emotional Colors emerging the more you listen, react, and commit to your character's needs? If so, record these discoveries in the last column marked Emotional Colors.

Try This:

Once your score sheet is complete for the scene, move beyond merely reading the scene out loud. Get up and explore how the Emotion Tactics and Subtext Statements affect your behavior. Use this acknowledgement as your way of staging or blocking a scene. Hand copies of your beat sheet to two other people, or side coaches. Each side coach will focus on one actor in the scene and call out the actor's score sheet choices while the actors are playing the scene. This works as an immediate reminder for the actor to embody the score. Too often actors will make intellectual choices on paper but not fully apply them in the scene. Or actors will feel the need to block a scene before acting it out, but the imposed blocking does not make sense to the character's motivations and behavior. By using emotions and Subtext Statements as clues for behavior and movement, the staging will emerge organically. A side coach reminds you of your score while acting, so you can feel how they work in the moment. Side coaches should keep calling out Emotion Tactics and Subtext Statements in a beat until they are convinced the actor is actually applying the choices. (Read more about Side Coaching at the end of the Manifestation Chapter.)

Applying an Emotion Approach

If you would like to use an Emotion Approach as the MVP for your acting, follow these steps:

1. Read and investigate the entire script for clues to your character's personality, feelings, and behaviors.

2. Determine your character's three emotional layers: (1) primary, (2) social mask, and (3) shadow self. Practice embodying these layers, to build a physical characterization.

3. Break your scenes into beats, and after determining your character's perspective on each beat, as well as the arc of the scene, assign Emotion Tactics and Subtext Statements.

4. Go over all the checklists for establishing beats, Emotion Tactics, and Subtext Statements to check your final work.

5. Rehearse your scenes applying Emotion Tactics and Subtext Statements,

and acknowledge moments of emotional reactions, Emotional Colors, or the Button, as well. (*see Actions Chapter for information on the Button*)

6. Invite a Side Coach to watch and remind you of your Emotion Tactics and Subtext Statements (*see Manifestation Chapter for more information on side coaching*)

7. Once the scene is memorized and rehearsed several times with the Emotion approach, check to see that aspects of Thought and Action have also clearly manifested in your performance. If not, apply exercises and techniques from those chapters to help bring these elements into your acting work.

Summary of Emotions

Can you now see how important it is to recognize that your body is an emotionally expressive canvas, containing layers that build from yourself, your character, the text, and the given circumstances around you in the performance? Can you also recognize how Emotion Tactics, Emotional Colors, and Subtext Statements assist you in consciously navigating and building the dramatic action of a play? Learning emotional awareness methods will help you deliver greater nuance to your acting, create clearer beat shifts, provide conscious control, and develop a clearer understanding of your own personal expression.

This chapter introduces the basic tools of scoring and preparing for rehearsals with an emotional approach. Later exercises will provide you with more tools for embodying these choices and help you align both the actor and the character together in one, cohesively expressive instrument. By studying and refining this skill of emotional expression, you can make this approach look like your own personal instinct or talent. Stanislavski says that in the end, at the final culmination of the actor's work, "artistic emotion is weighed not in pounds but in ounces."[23] Applying emotions to your acting does not necessarily mean you are an actor expressing your craft "full of sound and fury" but that you have reached a mature and refined understanding of how to express the many intricate levels of your character's feelings, reactions, and actions.

---

23. Ibid, 181.

In summary, Emotions in the TEAM are the character's, and many times the actor's, feelings that arise from reacting to internal thoughts, external given circumstances, and the character's conscious application of emotional states and behaviors. This includes reflections of character perspective and personality, reactions to Subtext Statements, Emotional Colors, and Emotion Tactics.

Further Study

Building A Character, by Constantine Stanislavski

Creating a Role, by Constantine Stanislavski

Sanford Meisner on Acting, by Sanford Meisner & Dennis Longwell

The Alba of Emotions, by Dr. Susana Bloch

"*Neither evening dress nor Greek tunic can hide from the audience the impression the body makes from the stage.*"

— Michael Chekhov

"*An Ounce of BEHAVIOR is Worth a Pound of WORDS.*"

— Sanford Meisner

Chapter 4

Actions

Action *(noun): Behavior, conduct, style of movement, a function of the body or one of its parts, an act of will, an actor's deportment or expression by means of attitude, voice and gesture.*[24]

Actions encompass many aspects of acting. The character's state of being is displayed through postural shifts, gestures, and minute muscular movements revealing how a character thinks, feels, and reacts to others. Tactics, blocking, and activities are also actions that exhibit valuable information. The category of Actions is often referred to as *acting choices* made by the performer to express the character's thoughts, needs, personality and emotions. This chapter will address Actions by discussing action tactics, general muscle movements, postural attitudes, and use of gesture and movement.

As you read on and learn more about how actions affect acting, consider this: If you had no words to express your character's feelings or needs, how would you get this across to others? The answer is in the actions.

Action Choices

Body language has the strongest impact on communication effectiveness. Our expressive bodies carry and deliver messages of our needs and desires with every move and sound we make. Michael Chekhov, the acting teacher known for

24. "Dictionary.com," accessed September 1, 2012, http://dictionary.reference.com.

creating Psychological Gestures, uses the term "will" to represent the character's need and objective. Within an explanation of the will, he says, "Out of this stirred will, all action, all 'business,' every gesture emerges on the stage, just as in life."[25] Considering the infinite choices we have with our posture, gestures, and activities, we can recognize that this part of the acting process allows for the greatest amount of personal creativity and craft. These choices often take the form of Action Tactics and behavior. There are countless action choices available to you for creating a vibrant and unique character, pulsing with multiple levels of action.

Think about what it would be like to watch a scene performed twice, with the same given circumstances, blocking, objectives, scenery, costumes, and directing. However, before the second presentation, one actor replaces another in a role. The second scene will be distinctly different if the new actor is truly making unique choices in Action Tactics and behavior. For the same reason we enjoy watching different athletes run the same course, seeing a classic movie remade by new actors, or even hearing individual family members retell the same family story, we appreciate the unique way in which different people portray events, through their own perspectives. This is true for the actor from moment to moment, scene to scene, and script to script. Your distinctive perspective and behavior shapes the style of action in the scene and in the entire script. Plays and movies depict the extraordinary, not the ordinary. Audiences attend live theatre and watch movies time and time again for this reason. Therefore, you must learn to make choices that are extraordinary as well.

A seasoned actor will most likely apply dynamic choices automatically, stemming from years of experience and training—much like an experienced driver who no longer has to think about every tactical move made in a car while navigating through traffic, new cities, unexpected obstacles, and varying weather conditions. In contrast, the beginning driver must gradually learn these skills and practice them under the guidance of a good instructor or through the examples of other seasoned drivers. There are some naturally talented actors who select unique choices instinctively or pick up skills easily by watching others. Unfortunately, if these actors don't learn some of the basic building blocks of actions, when they are met with unusually challenging roles, they will not have the tools to rise to the occasion as a trained actor would. Chekhov also warns these actors, "Only gestures that are properly done can arouse the actor's will. He has to learn and practice making such gestures in order to be able to apply

---

25. Chekhov, *On the Technique of Acting*, 38.

them later on to the professional work."[26] By learning about, and then practicing these techniques, they will eventually become instinctive. The experienced actor may also want to return to the basics of action choices in order to refine or challenge habitual choices. Acting is a craft, and as with any craft, it takes time to hone the skills required to do it well.

As you read through the following pages, keep in mind this process is broken down into specific steps with extensive checklists and vocabulary lists to assist a method that will eventually become second nature. In the future you will only need to revisit these steps and lists occasionally, like the seasoned actor mentioned previously.

Applying Action Tactics

The Emotions chapter provided lessons on breaking a scene into beats and assigning Emotion Tactics. These same beats can also be scored with Action Tactics. Action Tactics are the small actions characters use in order to achieve Scene Objectives. They are physical tools to accomplish a job.

[**Examples**] Compare this to a time when you had a difficult repair job to do. You first thought one tool was necessary to complete the job, but as you started working on the project you ran into minor complications or obstacles that made the first tool you chose inadequate for the job. So you selected a second tool and worked with that until you ran into another minor obstacle, and then picked a third tool and so on.

Now look at a scene in the same way. Your character approaches the scene with an objective, essentially a job that must be accomplished. She selects a tool, or tactic, believing it will work well in the first beat of the scene, the first step in accomplishing the job. Soon enough she is met with some kind of obstacle. She determines her first tool isn't getting her where she needs to go and she switches tools, or tactics. However, a new complication rises—a new subject or action created

26. Ibid, 39.

by others in the scene— and she chooses a different tool to deal with the new situation, or new beat.

These simple examples lay out the entire process of scoring a scene for Action Tactics. The tool comparison helps you see the reasoning for selecting Action Tactics to support the overall action, the objective. Now, the creative part: What tools do you select, and why?

Selecting Action Tactics

Action Tactics are selected by assigning an Action Word to the beat. You already know how to select an Action Word from the Thoughts chapter. As long as the word is active (Remember to steer away from such internal actions as *to be, to know, to wish,* etc.), there is a great deal of freedom available in action choices. Since tactics are meant as temporary tools, used for a brief amount of time, you have a bit more liberty in selecting tactical Action Words. For example, Action Tactics can *intimidate, badger, avoid,* etc. These words do not imply a final goal or objective. An Action Tactic is used until it becomes useless; then a new tactic is chosen. The new tactical choice remains the choice of the actor.

Have you ever heard the saying, "Doing the same action over and over again, but expecting a different result is the true definition of insanity"? If a character uses the same tactic and is not able to overcome obstacles or get closer to a victory, he can appear trapped in a state of repetition with no advancement, like the broken record stuck on one track. Selecting varying tactics to accomplish an urgent objective is an important element in creating dramatic action. Like the handyman who constantly builds his collection of tools in order to be prepared for all the varying jobs he must accomplish, the actor can do the same.

Action Tactic Variations in *The Importance of Being Earnest*

Read the following scene between Jack and Algernon from *The Importance of Being Earnest* by Oscar Wilde.[27] Then consider Algernon's Action Tactic

---

27. "Simply Scripts," last modified September 28, 2009, Oscar Wilde, *The Importance of Being Earnest*, (Public Domain), http://www.simplyscripts.com/plays_i_z.html.

options (a) or (b) for the first two beats. How might these choices introduce a different scene and mood? What tactics might you follow with in beats 3 and 4?

Beat #	Lines from Script	Action Tactic
1	ALGERNON. My dear fellow, the way you flirt with Gwendolen is perfectly disgraceful. It is almost as bad as the way Gwendolen flirts with you. JACK. I am in love with Gwendolen. I have come up to town expressly to propose to her.	*(a) to tease* *(b) to harass*
2	ALGERNON. I thought you had come up for pleasure? . . . I call that business. JACK. How utterly unromantic you are! ALGERNON. I really don't see anything romantic in proposing. It is very romantic to be in love. But there is nothing romantic about a definite proposal. Why, one may be accepted. One usually is, I believe. Then the excitement is all over. The very essence of romance is uncertainty. If ever I get married, I'll certainly try to forget the fact. JACK. I have no doubt about that, dear Algy. The Divorce Court was specially invented for people whose memories are so curiously constituted. ALGERNON. Oh! There is no use speculating on that subject. Divorces are made in Heaven – [JACK puts out his hand to take a sandwich. ALGERNON at once interferes.]	*(a) to complain* *(b) to scar*

TEAM for Actors

Beat #	Lines from Script	Action Tactic
3	Please don't touch the cucumber sandwiches. They are ordered specially for Aunt Augusta. [Takes one and eats it.] JACK. Well, you have been eating them all the time. ALGERNON. That is quite a different matter. She is my aunt. [Takes plate from below.] Have some bread and butter. The bread and butter is for Gwendolen. Gwendolen is devoted to bread and butter. JACK. [Advancing to table and helping himself.] And very good bread and butter it is too.	(a)_____ (b) _____
4	ALGERNON. Well, my dear fellow, you need not eat as if you were going to eat it all. You behave as if you were married to her already. You are not married to her already, and I don't think you ever will be. JACK. Why on earth do you say that? ALGERNON. Well, in the first place girls never marry the men they flirt with. Girls don't think it right. JACK. Oh, that is nonsense! ALGERNON. It isn't. It is a great truth. It accounts for the extraordinary number of bachelors that one sees all over the place.	(a)_____ (b) _____

Suppose the actor playing Algernon chose to play the first beat with the tactic *to tease*. With this light and friendly tactic, he chooses to start off the scene in a jovial mood. Then when Jack shifts the beat by announcing his proposal to Gwendolen, Algernon responds with the new tactic, *to complain*. The mood

140

immediately shifts from the implied jovial attitude into a downward turn of sour grapes. Such an approach to this scene would make Algernon appear as pouting, wounded, and insecure.

Now imagine the scene beginning in a different way, with Algernon starting the scene off in a foul mood and using the tactic *to harass*. The scene would begin with an immediate attack on Jack about his flirting with Gwendolen. Then, when Jack announces the proposal, Algernon uses the tactic *to scar*. This antagonistic tactic creates intense conflict and displays an Algernon who is furious about the news of the proposal.

Both approaches are possible and can be played with the given circumstances of the scene and play. Which choice do you think is more interesting? Which choice would lend itself more to a comedy, and which would better serve a drama? The possible combinations of tactics from beat-to-beat are endless, allowing a great deal of creativity for the actor and the director.

How would you complete the Action Tactics in the last two beats for Algernon in versions (a) and (b) in this scene? If you were playing Jack, how might you respond to receiving these Action Tactics? What tactics are possible for Jack's beats in the scene, and how might they vary from version (a) to version (b)?

[Example] Action Tactics for the Open Scene

The same open scene used in the Emotions chapter on beat identification follows. Approach the scene with character A's objective, *to get B to lend me the jacket.*

To help you imagine the circumstances, let's say that A is in the lobby of the restaurant, having just been denied access because he is not properly attired. His date is looking at him with great disappointment. Character A sees B, an old acquaintance, who is leaving the restaurant, having already eaten in this prestigious setting. Character A proceeds with his objective *to get B to lend me the jacket.* Notice how the beat subtext, introduced in the Emotions chapter, reinforces the tone of the Action Tactic.

Lines	Shift Subtext	Action Tactic
A: Hi. B: Hello.	"I haven't seen you in a while!"	to lure
A: Great outfit. B: Thanks.	"That jacket would fit me perfectly."	to flatter
A: Where did you get it? B: It's my own.	"Is this a rental?"	to delve
A: Your own? B: Yes. Mine. A: Wow! B: Thanks. A: I mean it. B: Well – again, thanks.	"Perfect for lending!"	to praise
A: So? I was wondering... B: Wondering? A: If you could...	"Let's get this awkward request over with."	to entreat
B: Really? A: Do you mind?	"Don't make me beg in front of my date!"	to plead
B: No. A: No? .... Or No?	"You don't really mean – No."	to coax
B: No. A: All right then. B: Ok.	"What a selfish bastard!"	to recoil

Try This:

After selecting new objectives for the open scene, break the scene into beats and assign your own Shift Subtext Statements and Action Tactics. See how many different tactical choices you can come up with for one scene using the same objective. By doing this, you will learn how to vary your choices, even under the same objective.

Without disclosing your objective or tactical choices beforehand, rehearse this scene with a scene partner and test your choices. Carry your score sheet with you in the scene, so your statements and tactics are readily available to reference as you work. Notice how these choices feel for you as you play the character, but also watch your scene partner's reactions as you try one tactic after another.

Which tactics get the best results? Which tactics create unique situations or reactions that you did not expect? Be sure to follow up this rehearsal with some good discussion with your scene partner, learning your scene partner's perspective about being on the receiving end of your choices.

To Question the Questioning

I am directing Tennessee William's short play, 27 Wagons Full of Cotton. *The play depicts the lives of private cotton gin owners at a time when such gins were being pushed out of business by large companies. The play reeks of violence in its opening scene, revealing a cotton gin owner, Jake, who intentionally blows up the gin of his competition while also physically abusing and threatening his wife, Flora, into fearful obedience. Soon after the play sets up the abusive husband and wife relationship, the character of Silva arrives to increase the intensity of the play's imposing doom.*

Silva is the supervisor for the competing cotton gin company, now forced to bring 27 wagons of cotton to Jake for ginning until their own gin is fixed. Silva suspects that the husband is the culprit in the gin's destruction. While Silva is left alone with Jake's wife, who attempts to keep him company on their porch while her husband gins the cotton, Silva conducts his own investigation of the situation.

Silva's character is written with lines that reveal a man full of braggadocio and allure, and yet he openly displays an undercurrent of menacing violence. He flirts, flashes his belly to show his dark Italian skin, and tells Flora he likes her. Meanwhile he interrogates and pushes her, swats at her with his riding crop and spins her on the porch swing until she is dizzy from the movement and the inquisition. As the play progresses, Silva determines Jake's guilt and eventually imposes his sentence and violent punishment for the crime.

While working on the scene between Flora and Silva, I notice the actor playing Silva is coming across as very quiet, flat, and one-noted in his action choices. Throughout the scene Silva questions Flora about Jake's activities during the night of the gin fire. Although the scene is written with many questions from Silva, and with short avoiding answers from Flora, the action in this scene could have more variations beyond generalized questions and answers.

I ask the actor playing Silva if he assigned Action Tactics to this scene. He says that he did and was working on applying them. I suggest that the actor make those action choices bigger, by embodying them more. Perhaps this was the reason the scene was lacking intensity and variation. Some actors will make intellectual choices but not embody them enough, keeping them trapped in their minds and unaware of how to place them in their posture, gestures, and activities. I run the scene again, but the scene still comes across quiet, passive, and lacking the bravado this character could have.

I ask the actor to show me his scene score, and specifically his Action Tactics. His score is filled with the Action Tactic, "to question." At least every third beat has this tactic. Here the actor is taking the question mark at the end of his lines literally, and seeing only the one option for an Action Tactic. I talk to the actor about all the ways in which a person could question and what motives lie behind questions. I then point out how selecting dynamic Action Tactics could make the *questioning far more active, turning those simple questions into true tactical maneuvers. We discuss some examples of this: to interrogate, to muse, to ridicule, to tease, to flirt, and to threaten.*

I encourage the actor to reassign every beat with a new Action Tactic before our next rehearsal. His assignment is to see if he can completely discard the tactic, "to question" before his next rehearsal. He has a lot of actor homework to catch up with but the payoff for such diligence to Action Tactics will not only increase the quality of his performance, but provide greater tension, mystery, and far more obstacles for the actress playing Flora.

Weak Choices

Selecting Action Tactics for each beat is an opportunity to put your unique imprint on the scene. Selecting obvious tactics, with little to no depth implied, creates dull performances.

[**Example**] In the open scene explored earlier, there are a number of beats where a character is asking a question—made clear by the script's use of a question mark. Similar to the actor playing Silva in *27 Wagons Full of Cotton*, many actors will simply use the Action Tactic to question in these beats. There is no real choice made by the actor here; it was made by the playwright. Merely stating, "to question" whenever one sees a question mark, minimizes the strength the actor can bring to the scene.

Consider this: How many different ways can one ask a question? You could *plead, beg, inquire, quiz, ponder, interrogate, interpolate, badger, nurture, persuade, guide, invite, lead, hustle, convince, attract*, etc. The same holds true if you see a statement followed by an exclamation point. A weak choice for an Action Tactic would be to assume the tactic is *to yell*. An exclamatory statement can be delivered with so many other subtext implications, depending on the actor's choice in the delivery of the beat. The tactic could be *to inspire, praise, empower, radiate, goad, reject, reveal, incite, enchant, demand*, etc. Learn to see the difference between a generalized action—*to question, to yell, to quote, to think*—and a more specific action verb implying action, subtext, and even emotion.

Another sign of a weak choice is an Action Tactic that provides emotion but, no action. Many Action Words can imply an emotional state while also steering an action. Look at some of the Action Tactics given as examples above in order to replace *to question. Interrogate* and *badger* imply a hint of anger whereas, *nurture, guide,* and *invite* involve some tenderness. Then the words *hustle* and *attract* have the possibility of some sexual connotations. However, words like *sob, laugh, scream, shriek, wail, moan, sigh, giggle, hum,* and *gasp* only support the character's own emotional state of being. They are not actions directed toward another in pursuit of an objective. Although they sound dynamic because they refer to an emotional state, these words are not strong choices for Action Tactics.

Remember, Action Tactics are "the small actions characters use in order to obtain their Scene Objectives." The weak choices mentioned here only provide emotional reactions or repeat the action stated by stage directions prescribing line delivery. When initially selecting an Action Tactic, stay away from words that do not provide actions devoted to obtaining your objective or accomplishing a job.

Varying Action Tactics

Tactics assigned to each beat should be new actions attempted. Too often I will read an actor's scene score and see two or three beats in a row that have the same Action Tactic assigned. With so many actions available, why keep selecting the same exact one? There is quite a difference between *to inspire, to praise,* and *to empower,* even though all three imply that you are trying to raise the spirits of the person to whom you are talking. Likewise, *to goad, to incite,* and *to demand* all could be working toward getting someone to take action for you; however, each has a varying degree of intensity, subtle differences in intentional actions, and slight shifts in personal motivations.

When selecting tactics for each beat, make sure you have a new choice for the next beat and be sure you understand the definition of the word used. Look it up in the dictionary if you are not sure. If you have a tendency to use the same words over and over again, look up those words in a thesaurus to find variations, and then make sense of their differences in actions. By doing this, you will expand your own action vocabulary and improve your acting skills one new Action Word at a time.

Exercise
Identify the Weak Tactics

Below is the same open scene used previously. It keeps the same Subtext Statement for character (A), yet new tactics have been assigned. Each of these new Action Tactics are weak choices. Can you identify why they are weak?

Lines	Shift Subtext	Action Tactic
A: Hi. B: Hello.	"I haven't seen you in a while!"	to shout(1)
A: Great outfit. B: Thanks.	"That jacket would fit me perfectly."	to state(2)
A: Where did you get it? B: It's my own.	"Is this a rental?"	to question(3)
A: Your own? B: Yes. Mine. A: Wow! B: Thanks. A: I mean it. B: Well – again, thanks.	"Perfect for lending!"	to question(4)
A: So? I was wondering... B: Wondering? A: If you could...	"Let's get this awkward request over with."	to ask(5)

Lines	Shift Subtext	Action Tactic
B: Really? A: Do you mind?	"Don't make me beg in front of my date!"	to whimper(6)
B: No. A: No? …. Or No?	"You don't really mean – No."	to exclaim(7)
B: No. A: All right then. B: Ok.	"What a selfish bastard!"	to snarl(8)

After identifying the weak tactical choices and the reasons why they are weak, replace the weak tactics with strong Action Tactics. Read the scene out loud, preferably with a scene partner, and test these choices. Go back and read the scene out loud with the weak choices and compare how the scene differs when stronger choices are made. Keep testing new strong choices in the scene and explore how much the scene can be improved by each new choice made.

Actions Used with Facades and Masks

When working on choosing Action Tactics for a scene this question often comes up: "If my character does not want to show how he truly feels, and instead wears a social mask or façade, are my tactics the façade or the truth?" This is an excellent question. So many characters, as well as people in real life, won't reveal their true desires easily. The honest desires, needs, and motivations of the character are often hidden, covered up by intentional actions used to get what they want. These actions, by design, cleverly disguise their desires and protect perceived vulnerabilities. In fact, many of your most intriguing characters are so compelling because they are not revealing their truths too easily, and so the audience is constantly drawn in, trying to figure out what is really motivating the character's actions. For example, in a mystery or thriller story, the covert "bad guy," who is not revealed until the end, relies on deception. His honest desires are revealed occasionally, just often enough to keep the audience and other characters looking for subtle clues left by these brief truthful revelations.

A good rule of thumb to use here is, Action Tactics are the character's conscious actions. The character is quite mindful of what she is doing and what she is revealing by using these actions. If your character is purposely putting on a figurative mask, then the tactics chosen would support this mask. For example, if your character wants to destroy her co-worker so she can have his job but not let her co-worker know what she is up to, then she wears the mask of the *good friend* when she is around him, when in fact she is his enemy. However, if your character is interacting with someone with whom she feels she can be honest and vulnerable, and chooses to drop the façade, then the tactics chosen would support this as well. That same character may be in a different scene with her trusted friend, confessing her plan to destroy her co-worker and fully revealing all her feelings and intentions.

Reactions and Discoveries

You may ask, "Then where are the subtle crumbs of truth dropped when my character is wearing her façade?" This is, once again, a good question to consider when making choices of action and Emotion Tactics. In daily interactions with others we have actions and then reactions. Too often an actor focuses only on the actions and not on the reactions, so much so that a common saying has passed down from generations of actors, reminding actors to react: "Acting is 50% acting and 50% reacting." You can also look at it this way: every action has a reaction. However there is an extra step occurring between the action and the reaction that is often overlooked as well. It is the act of interpretation. Even when someone is wearing a conscious social mask, the moment of interpretation or what can also be called a moment of discovery, is when flashes of truth can be witnessed.

The basic elements of the interpersonal communication process include three steps: (1) receiving messages from either an outside source (the actions of another) or an inside source (your thoughts); (2) decoding the messages for personal meanings; and (3) sending messages (your words and behaviors) that express the reaction. For acting purposes, you can break the process down into:

(1) Reception

(2) Interpretation

(3) Action

All three steps occur very quickly—appearing instantaneous—with very little hesitation between steps. The second step of Interpretation often looks like truthful flashes of personal discovery, recognition, acknowledgement, processing, or the "think before you speak" moment. We are constantly interpreting what we read, hear, feel, and think before we act. You are experiencing this Interpretation step constantly as you read through this book, make personal discoveries, and consider theories and techniques. The Interpretation step can be so subtle that you may not even recognize it yourself.

When acting a role, it is important to recognize this step in your character's behavior and to acknowledge when this interpretation might be more obvious than at other times. We will use the term Discovery Moment when the interpretation process is more obvious and provides a pivotal turning point in your character's behavior. A fellow acting teacher I worked with years ago used to call out, "Welcome to the Discovery Channel!" when he saw an actor recognize and embody this behavior between Reception and Action.

The Discovery Moment often occurs right before a beat shift, signaling that the character has a new thought or idea. This does not mean that a Discovery Moment is required before each beat. This could end up producing a very predictable, and most likely comical, style of delivery. However, Discovery Moments could occur during a reaction where a big surprise is revealed, a new idea surfaces, or a character is caught off guard. The options in your acting communication process might now map more like this:

(1)   Reception

	Thinking/Processing		**Instinctive**
(2)	Interpretation	OR	Discovery
	Conscious Act		**Impulsive Act**
(3)	Action	OR	Reaction

When you consider basic brain activity and how it triggers actions, the Discovery Moments can also be described as our limbic response. The limbic system reflects instinctive, emotional, and life-sustaining responses. These responses would, by their very nature, reflect truthful flashes of how we really feel about another person, our environment, or our thoughts. How often have you been in a conversation with someone and reacted to what they were saying before they finished? Continuously, right? These are honest impulses in the form of reactions. We are not just talking about interrupting and overlapping dialogue. Although the interruptions happen as well, the point is we are reacting nonverbally throughout the interpersonal communication. Our reactions are in our body gestures, posture, facial expressions, movements, activities, tone of voice, and even eye directions. These reactions speak great truths about what the character is feeling.

This interpersonal process is spontaneous, truthful, and ongoing. The reaction is an impulsive, physical and emotional action. An example of an instinctive and truthful response from everyday life is when you hear an unexpected loud noise. Your limbic system reacts with a quick fearful movement, either jumping, pulling back, or even flashing the eyes. Once your neocortex, or the "thinking brain," catches up with the situation, you can then execute conscious logical actions in the situation.

[**Example**] When you hear something that saddens you, you may find that your body quickly reacts with your eyes pinching upward with a sympathetic look, as you sigh at hearing the news. Then you realize you don't want to show this sadness or increase your own level of upset, so you consciously choose to adopt a serious and thoughtful stance. This reaction/action process includes instinctive and conscious actions and may look like this:

First Phase

(1)   Reception: *Sad news received from co-worker*

(2)   Instinctive Act\Discovery: *I feel sad*

(3)   Impulsive Act\Reaction: *Instinctive sad behavior*

Second Phase

(1)   Reception: *My thoughts interpret that my behavior makes my co-worker more sad.*

(2)   Thinking\Interpretation: *I think I should adopt a more supportive behavior.*

(3)   Conscious Act\Action: *I consciously project serious concern for the situation.*

If you look at times in your own life when you were caught off guard by someone else's actions, how did you react? Are you aware that you most likely reacted with a very honest, yet quick, action? Your reaction was a reflection of your true feelings about the information you were receiving. Then, you might just as quickly have formulated a response that you felt better suited the situation. The response you formulated was your conscious action—or tactic, for the situation. The reaction you initially gave was your impulsive truthful response to the situation, exposing your interpretation or Discovery Moment.

Scoring Reactions and The Button

The same interpersonal communication exchange holds true for acting out interactions in a script. Your character has the opportunity to react truthfully and then make many choices about how to express ideas and behaviors in line with her objective. In order to provide a tangible process for scoring your script with Actions and Reactions, use the Action Tactics as your character's conscious objectives for each beat of the script. Then, look at your scene partner's lines for specific moments where your own character would make a discovery and act impulsively. Mark that area in the script by highlighting the word or phrase your scene partner says that initiates your reaction, or by placing a large dot or asterisk there to point it out to yourself during rehearsals. This moment of reaction, found in the other person's lines or actions, is often referred to as The Button. It literally pushes your character's buttons, initiating an impulsive response of truthful behavior.

Actions

[**Example**] Let's look at a basic scenario of a character (A) who plans to destroy her co-worker (B). Imagine the following dialogue between the two:

A: Don't worry. I'll take care of it.

B: What are you up to?

A: What do you mean?

If Character A is wearing a friendly façade in order to accomplish the object, *to destroy my co-worker,* she will approach this short exchange with the tactics, *to persuade with confidence.* However, she is caught off guard by the line from Character B. Perhaps her subtext in that moment is "Does he know my plan?", so she responds very briefly in fear and worry that she has been found out. She then regains her composure and asks the last line, applying the tactic *to probe with suspicion.* Her reaction of fear is between the beats of action, before she probes for more information.

The exchange between characters above might look like this in a script for Character A:

Lines	Shift Subtext	Action	Emotion
A: Don't worry. I'll take care of it.	"Trust me."	To persuade	Confident
B: What are you up to?		*[Subtle Fear Reaction]*	
A: What do you mean?	"Does he know my plan?"	To probe	Suspicious

Notice, your score sheet can provide an action, reaction, and discovery road map of the scene. You will need to decide whether your character is in a situation where she can respond truthfully or if she must consciously keep up a façade to serve her objective. The reactions will reveal the truths of your character, unless her defenses are fully up and guarded against all possible actions from opposing forces.

Automatic Auto-Da-Fe

While directing Tennessee Williams' short play, Auto-Da-Fe, *our two-actor cast made good use of subtext, buttons, and reactions. The play takes place on the porch of Madame Duvenet's boarding house. The entire action of the play is a conversation between her and her adult son Eloi. Her son is trying to make a confession to his mother about a personal investigation he has been making concerning a certain young man, a photo of two nude men, and a possibly conspiring boarder who lives in their house. The dialogue is riddled with innuendo, suspicious questioning, and defensive reactions between two people who care very much for each other but feel terribly misunderstood. The play ends quite dramatically in a life threatening situation.*

The actor playing Eloi is a trained dancer, and because of his experience in movement he decides to use an Action Tactic approach, thinking this would help him connect the best with the character. The woman playing Madame Duvenet is trained in Alba Emoting and decides to approach the character first with Emotion Tactics.

As we rehearse the play and discuss the character's objectives, victories, and the possibility of secrets, the actors find themselves struggling to embody the reaction aspects of the play. The play is coming across at this point as a tedious question-and-answer dialogue. I feared if we did not enliven it with passionate reactions, imbued with relationship history, the play could fall into a dull scene leading to an unexplained dramatic ending. The actors confess all their choices so far feel like self-imposed movements and behaviors that, although interesting to do and to watch, do not yet seem to fully reveal all the layers we found through our table talk sessions at the beginning of rehearsal. We acknowledge that more embodiment techniques as well as more intricate reaction scoring are probably needed.

I encourage the actors to add Shift Subject Statements to their work. Since the actors are off book (lines memorized) at this point, we are able to run an exercise where the actors can impulsively speak their subtext out loud, in-between the scripted lines. They proceed to practice this approach, mumbling subtext to themselves, yelling out their truths to the universe, or actually saying what they are really thinking to the other character's face. The exercise turns into a riotous shouting and pouting match, which immediately helps the actors embody many honest reactions, and also colors their tactical actions with emotions.

I then ask each actor to listen to the other character's lines for The Button that makes them want to react honestly. We run another form of exercise where each actor now has permission to interrupt the other at any time their button is pushed, but they may speak their scripted lines only, infusing them with the feelings and honesty of the subtext. With this technique, the play quickly reaches new heights in acting work, displaying the kind of conversation that we often see in real life between people who know each other extremely well. The scenes have occasional moments of overlapping lines but also moments of silent tension. The characters talk over each other for some lines, raising their volume, in hopes of being heard and understood, until another button is pushed that either causes the other to stop and listen, walk away in disgust, or contemplate how to word their next thought, carefully. These actions and reactions now have layers of history, love, frustration, pain, and desire in the lines, between the lines, and in all the displayed behaviors. The play is now very much alive and passionately urgent.

Making Strong Choices

Making strong tactical choices is a skill where an actor can excel if he constantly asks, "Did the choice work well or not?" Most of the time, the actor can rely on a rehearsal process and the guidance of a director to steer toward choices more suitable for the final performance. However, for those using the TEAM for film acting, it is important to realize that film actors have very little rehearsal time, if any. Film actors are often required to make the strongest most creative choice on the spot in a shoot, and they should have a few other back-up choices ready to go for the "next take," for time is money on a film shoot. Additionally, when an actor is auditioning for any role—stage or film—he is observed for his ability to make dynamic choices right off the bat, so the director knows she can rely on him to be a self-guided actor. The less a director is needed to guide an actor in his acting craft, the more prone she is to cast him. Therefore, an actor's ability to make strong unique choices in the moment, in support of the script, is a valuable skill to hone for the success of any type of acting career.

Notice, choices are not referred to as being right or wrong. The choice of tactics is very much up to interpretation. There really isn't a right or wrong to such selections. However, if the tactic is common, trite, weak, inactive, too predictable, or completely out of line with the given circumstances of the script, then it is a weak choice, or simply doesn't work well. On the other hand, if the tactic is fresh, active, unique, unexpected, provides levels to the performance, supplies a new perspective, and is still in support of the given circumstances of the script and directing concept, then it is a strong choice. Simply put, it works well!

Unique tactical maneuvers are celebrated throughout our history. Leaders who use unpredictable wartime strategies to accomplish their goals in order to win at any cost, make history. Inventors who create new ways of solving problems with their inventions are using groundbreaking tactics to win their places in the history books. Artists who use new materials and fresh ways of looking at things often find themselves the talk of the town, sometimes for ages. The same is true for actors who catch the attention of their audiences with unique approaches to their roles leading to award-winning performances. How does one learn to do this? If it isn't already an automatic instinct within you, it takes practice to develop this skill. The following are some guidelines to consider as you develop your skills in making dynamic tactical choices.

Checklist for Choosing Action Tactics

☐ Use specific Action Words to title your tactics; avoid generalized verbs.

☐ Make sure each new beat has a distinctly new Action Tactic.

☐ Build your Action Word vocabulary to encompass a wide range of actions, and fully understand the meaning of the word used.

☐ Steer clear of words that are highly intellectual, simply emotional, or existential.

☐ Use your Action Words to reflect your character's conscious choices of action toward the Scene Objective.

Developing Your Action Vocabulary

This process is similar to when you learn a new language. You may study lists of words to memorize and associate with your own native language. Eventually, with practice and immersion into the language and culture, the new language becomes habitual. In order to develop your Action Vocabulary for acting, keep a running list of Action Words for tactics in a journal or small notebook that you can keep with your script, just as you might keep a foreign language dictionary around to translate on the spot. As you develop your skills in selecting tactics, make note of the words you tend to use the most. Then start to take more risks with your choices, and challenge your perspective by forcing yourself to select different tactics, essentially building a broad and diverse Action Tactic Vocabulary for your work. At first this work will feel very time-consuming, but with practice and application, it will come easily to you, like the new language coming up when you need it, no longer requiring you to reach for that translation dictionary.

Postural Attitudes

Postural Attitudes are full body expressions of a person's feelings, mood, and personality. The word *attitude* can be defined as "position or posture of the body appropriate to or expressive of an action, emotion, etc."[28] The Action Tactic is an intellectual or psychological choice that must be put into action. The acting teacher Michael Chekhov said, "Each individual psychological state is always a combination of thoughts (or Images), Feelings, and Will-impulses."[29] He referred to gestural developments such as "the Gesture together with the Feelings connected with it" as the Psychological Gesture. It is the will-impulse that ignites these thoughts and feelings into action. Stanislavski referred to this process of postures and actions turned to living images of movement as, Physical Actions.

In Alba Emoting, Postural Attitudes[30] are an essential aspect of the basic emotion patterns. These postures are exhibited through the body's leaning directions, curve of the spine, tension or relaxation of muscles, weight distribution, and arm gestures. When learning Alba Emoting, one can spend years learning and perfecting control of the intricacies within each of these Postural Attitudes.

28. Dictionary.com (2012) http://dictionary.reference.com/
29. Chekhov, *On the Technique of Acting*, 59.
30. Susana Bloch, "Alba Emoting: A Psychophysiological Technique to Help Actors Create and Control Real Emotions," Theatre Topics, (1993).

However, actors can benefit from learning even the most generalized aspects of these postures, and their association to Action Tactics.

In order to simplify the study of Postural Attitudes, let's first consider very basic shifts in our posture that contribute to varying modes of expression. Changes of muscle tonicity— or the tension state of muscles— can move in two opposing directions: tension or relaxation.

Try This:

Take a moment and tense as many of your large muscle groups as possible. Hold that tension for a moment and explore how this affects your posture, movement, gestures, and also your mood. Then release the tension as much as you can. Experiment with how this also affects your overall posture and ability to move and express yourself. You probably noticed that there were varying degrees of tension and relaxation as you went from one polarity of muscle tonicity to the other, which shows the range possible between these two extreme states for variations of expression.

General Muscle Movements

In addition to our muscle tonicity, muscles also have general directions of movement, expressed in terms of opposites: (a) extend/flex, (b) abduct/adduct, (c) elevate/depress, and (d) internal/external rotation. Take a moment and explore these movements in a standing position:

[Examples]

a) **Extend/Flex:** Explore the difference between extending parts of your body like arms, legs, head, and hands. Then, try moving in an opposite direction of that extension and flex or bend these areas. How do you feel as you embody these opposite directions?

b) **Abduct/Adduct:** To abduct is to pull aspects of your body away from your midline, or center axis. Your spine is the marker for your body's midline. Try abducting your arms and legs away from the midline by raising your arms and spreading your legs. Now move in the opposite direction and adduct. What happens to your overall posture as you bring your arms and legs inward, close to your midline?

c) **Elevate/Depress:** How might you elevate the muscles in your shoulders? Perhaps lifting your shoulders upward? Do you notice other muscles in your rib cage and back moving along with this upward movement? Then depress the same muscles by either pushing them downward or by releasing the tension used to lift them and essentially give-in to gravity. How does this muscle depression affect how you stand, and how you feel? Does it feel different if you choose to push down rather than release tension?

d) **Internal/External Rotation:** What happens if you rotate your arms and legs internally, or in toward your chest and pelvis? Hold this for a moment and recognize how it affects your overall posture. Did your hands and feet move to accomplish this? Then rotate your arms and legs externally, perhaps by turning your hands and feet so the palms and toes face outward or away from the midline of your body.

These basic muscle movements directly affect the quality of our posture, movement, actions, and overall mood. As you explored the examples of muscle directions, did you notice any muscle tonicity changes associated with each exploration? When you tried these examples did you also sense changes in your overall mood or feelings as you went from one extreme movement to the next? The two areas of tonicity and general directional movements are interconnected, as are our postures, actions, and feelings.

Postural Attitudes and Emotions

Building upon the original Alba Emoting patterns and their Postural Attitudes, I have grouped the basic patterns into pairs that articulate these polarities between states of expression. Consider this polarity expressed in a line with an A representing one extreme and a B representing the opposite degree.

A: The A-state represents an attitude that has the least amount of tension coupled with muscle directional movement that exhibits an open and approachable Postural Attitude.

B: The B-state exemplifies postures that have the greatest degree of tension and/or uses general muscle movements that close the body off to others or make it unapproachable.

Some people might refer to these Postural Attitudes like this: A exhibits positive attributes, and B expresses negative states. However one prefers to view these expressive modes, it is important to recognize that they can be grouped into these primary categories of opposites, or cognate pairs. Minor changes of tension and directional movements can easily shift a person from expressing in an A-state to a B-state, or vice versa. It is also important to acknowledge that there are varying degrees of these states between their extremes.

Opposite States of Expressive Behavior

1A   1B

The posture of Tenderness (1A) is relaxed, open and tends to gaze forward, extending arms to adore or protect. Anger (1B) is expressed with tension and by moving forward, extending this tense posture toward the stimulus of the anger.

(1A) Tenderness
Relaxed Tonicity
Muscle Movements in Specific Areas:
Extend/Abduct/Depress
& External rotation

(1B) Anger
Tense Tonicity
Muscle Movements in Specific Areas:
Extend/Adduct/Elevate
& Internal rotation

2A   2B

Sensuality (2A) has a relaxed open posture, with muscles rotating outward for a posture that expresses openly receiving and acquiring that which it desires. Fear (2B) is exhibited with sudden and extreme tension of muscle movement rotating inward and pulling up and back, avoiding the object that instigates the fear.

<u>(2A) Sensuality</u>
Relaxed Tonicity
Muscle Movements in Specific Areas:
Extend/Abduct/Elevate
& External rotation

<u>(2B) Fear</u>
Tense Tonicity
Muscle Movements in Specific Areas:
Flex/Adduct/Elevate
& Internal rotation

3A   3B

Happiness (3A) is relaxed and yet elevates muscle movement, expressing lightness and bounce while placing attention on the subject or person that ignites this joyous feeling. Sadness (3B) has very little muscle tension and actually depresses the muscles downward while rotating the posture inward, closing its posture off to others.

(3A) Happiness
Relaxed Tonicity
Muscle Movements in Specific Areas:
Flex/Adduct/Elevate
& External rotation

(3B) Sadness
Relaxed Tonicity
Muscle Movements in Specific Areas:
Flex/Adduct/Depress
& Internal rotation

As you look at these opposites, it may not be immediately clear to you why some are expressed as opposites of each other. Beyond the postural degree changes in these patterns, a key aspect in Alba Emoting that clearly defines these opposites is their associated breathing patterns.[31] Although we won't go into this in detail in this book, you can explore some general breath aspects of Postural Attitudes on your own, like the one in the Try This that follows.

Try This:

While standing, look at an object across the room that is approximately at eye level. Breathe in and out of your nose, with your mouth closed.

As you look at this object, consider the muscles inside your nasal passage constricting and tensing as you breathe. Encourage other muscles on the outsides of your nose, and just under your eyes to also tense and adduct, or move inwards toward your nose.

Do you feel any degree of anger as you explore this? Varying levels of anger can be from low to high concentration, directness, assertiveness, seriousness, frustration, aggression, furiousness, and rage.

Then, while continuing your nose breathing, move your facial muscles in the opposite direction, by relaxing the muscle tonicity and abducting the muscles inside your nasal passage. Encourage the muscles located on the outside of your nose, your upper cheeks, and even those on the outsides of your eyes to abduct and elevate, moving outwards and upwards toward your ears.

Do the muscles around your cheeks and near the outsides of your mouth also want to move up and out toward the ears? Can you feel any degree of tenderness forming as you explore this opposite direction of movement and relax your breathing and muscle tonicity? Varying levels of tenderness can be peacefulness, ease, tranquility, and adoration.

---

31. Susana Bloch, Madeline Lemeignan, and Nancy Aguilera-Torres, "Specific Respiratory Patterns Distinguished Among Human Basic Emotions," International Journal of Psychophysiology," (1991).

Postural Attitudes as Embodied Actions

Postural Attitudes also affect activities, objectives and tactics. Common traits of the 1, 2, and 3 patterns express actions supporting these basic categories: (1) Giving, (2) Receiving, and (3) Reflecting states of being.

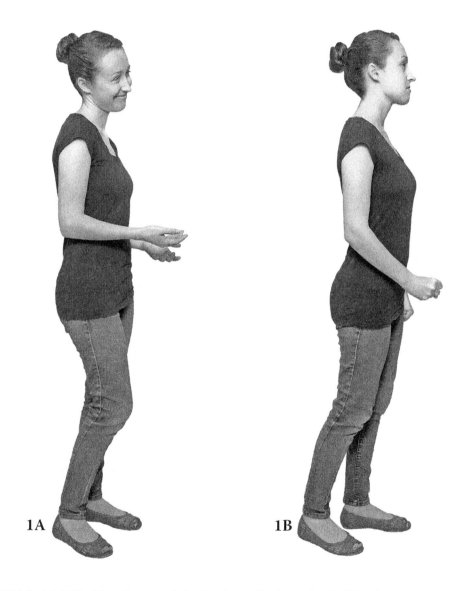

GIVING 1A/1B: The Postural Attitudes of 1A and 1B (Tenderness & Anger) are focused forward and the eye contact is placed on someone or something. Someone expressing Anger or Tenderness is in a Giving State of either giving love (1A) or giving their anger (1B).

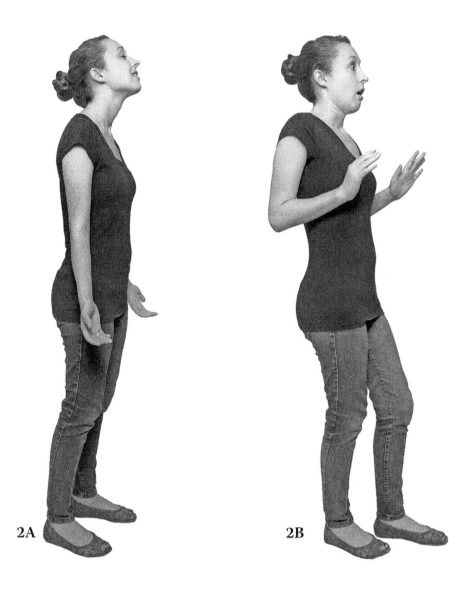

2A   2B

RECEIVING 2A/2B: The patterns of 2A and 2B (Sensuality & Fear) both have Postural Attitudes of leaning back in reaction to an external stimulus. These two postures are in Receiving states of something pleasant (2A) or shocking (2B).

The number/letter reference in these terms connects with the Emotion Tactics in the Emotions chapter. This way you might be able to recognize connections between similar categories of Action Tactics and Emotion Tactics.

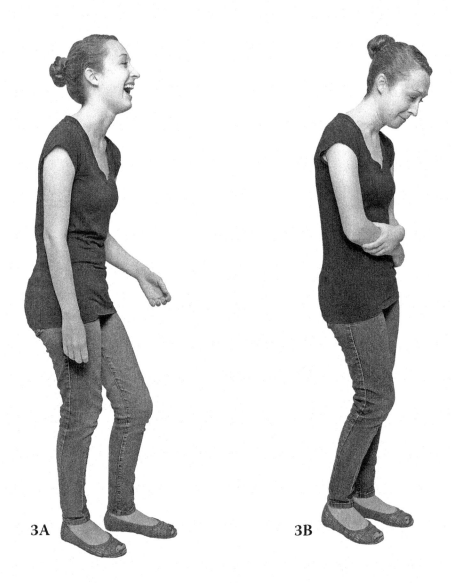

3A **3B**

REFLECTING 3A/3B: Attitudes of 3A and 3B (Happiness & Sadness) are often focused more on the state of being, or on feeling the emotion for one's self. Sadness (3B) closes the body off in order to explore this feeling, and Happiness (3A) opens up and invites the body to a Reflecting state, radiating joy outward.

These general categories of posture and movement are offered as a beginning step in embodying the myriad of Action Words possible. By categorizing them into Postural Attitudes, we can understand the core elements of posture and movement inherent within the term, which would then translate into actions.

If an Action Tactic is embodied, it becomes a physical attitude. Take that physical attitude and put it into motion, and you have gestures, blocking, and physical interactions with others.

Exercise
Applying Postural Attitudes to Activities and Interactions

Stand face to face with your scene partner. Select an object that you can pass back and forth between the two of you. Some ideal objects are those that are durable and soft—so you don't get carried away and hurt each other or the object. Some objects to try: a large bath towel or piece of fabric, a soft beach ball, or a pillow. Take turns exchanging the object between the two of you as you exercise the Postural Attitudes and observe their effect on activity, interaction, and posture.

(1B) Give forcefully while lifting the thorax and advancing with tension, eyes on the source of this tense state.

(1A) Give in a relaxed open and embracing state, eyes on the source of affection.

(2B) Receive with upward and backward tension and defensiveness, eyes and ears alerted toward the source of fear or surprise.

(2A) Receive by relaxing back and opening up the neck and thorax, reducing the need for sight and focusing on the other senses, like touch.

(3B) Reflecting inward and downward with a feeling of weighty inertia, eyes and gestures express the need for privacy.

(3A) Reflecting outward with a loose, light, and bouncy state, eyes and gestures want to share this state with others.

As you explored these postures, actions, and interactions how did they affect
• your handling of the object?
• your relationship to your partner?
• your movement and gestures?

Try adding the following to this exercise to investigate more action levels:
• A greater distance between you and your partner
• A specific activity, like folding the towel, bouncing the ball, or tossing the pillow to your partner
• A line of text to accompany the action like, "Here, take this," "I was told to give this to you," or "Do me a favor, and take this with you."

How did these new elements add to the range of expressive qualities possible within each Postural Attitude? Can you see how the Postural Attitudes can work as building blocks for scene activities, blocking, line expression, and physical interactions?

Posturing in 27 **Wagons Full of Cotton**

While I'm directing 27 Wagons Full of Cotton, *we stop to work on the scene between Jake and Silva when the husband is happily reaping the benefits of his competitor's burned down gin. Jake struts around his front yard, commenting on the big load of work he is going to do for Silva's company. He calls out his wife, proudly introduces her to Silva, and suggests that she keep him company while he [Jake] gins the cotton.*

The actor playing Jake likes to approach character development using Postural Attitudes and Action Tactics. This approach works very well for this domineering, boastful, yet playful character. The actor playing Jake also happens to be shorter in stature than the actress playing his wife, and considerably shorter than the actor playing Silva. Yet, it is clear to us that the character wants to be big, tall, and formidable.

I coach the actor on how to mix Giving 1B with Reflecting 3A: "In this scene I want you to lift yourself up, with every gesture, every attitude you project, intending to make yourself bigger, taller, and more important than Silva. Mix in some bounce in your step and in your gestures, and laugh when you can to reflect a mask of joy and ease." The actor applies these directions to his posture, gestures, and movements. He puffs up his chest, sticks out his chin, kicks his boots up with big straddling steps as he struts like a rooster in his yard and in front of his hen. When he shakes Silva's hand, he pulls his hand up high and shakes with a broad high pump. He throws out a tense laugh occasionally as his gestures flail broadly. At first we are all giggling at this comical display, knowing full well what he is attempting to do. But as the actor adjusts these big gestures into a reasonable level of body language intensity for Jake, the character comes across as confident, boastful, and on top of the world.

Later in the play, the actor playing Jake has another challenging scene. He returns to the front porch from a hard day's work ginning cotton. He is feeling full of himself, proud of how he managed to set up this sweet deal, as he sits on the steps of the front porch talking to his wife. The challenge in this scene is that although he is talking with his wife about his day's activities and her "visit" with Silva—he never really sees her clearly. He does not notice that she is bruised and that her skin is streaked with blood from Silva's vengeful abuse while Jake was out of sight. The actor struggles with this lack of observation; he does not understand how he cannot see that his wife has been beat up.

I coach the actor to approach the scene with Receiving 2A— opening up his posture and breath to drink in his success—but with reduced attention to sight: "Settle so far into yourself and into reveling in your success that you literally are counting wagons full of cotton in your head. The dollar signs that each wagon represents hang like veils before your eyes, and you can't understand why your wife is not thrilled as well." I encourage him to visualize more wagons full of cotton coming all summer long. I tell him, "It is ok to glance back at your wife occasionally, but you don't really see her, because her behavior and words are not matching your vision; they are an obstacle you must overcome as you attempt to get both of you invested in this vision."

The actor uses this imagery and the Action Tactics associated with Receiving 2A quite successfully. He even walks right past his wife as he goes into the house and tells her to get in the car, so they can go to town for some Cokes. The actress playing Flora uses an opposing objective, "See me!" throughout the scene. It tears her up to no end when he waltzes right by her, never noticing her terrible state, and then nonchalantly instructs her to go to the car. The play comes to an end as we watch Flora slowly and painfully work her way toward the car.

Postural Attitudes and Action Words

Postural Attitudes*
Giving (1A)
Giving (1B)
Receiving (2A)
Receiving (2B)
Reflecting (3A)
Reflecting (3B)

*These terms were created by Laura Bond, influenced by the Alba Emoting Technique.

Looking at the six Postural Attitudes, where would you place Action Tactics like: (a) *to soothe*, (b) *to reject*, (c) *to fight*, and (d) *to admire*? Say each of these tactics out loud as you allow your body to convey the meaning of the word with a full body gesture.

a) You might find that as you try *to soothe* someone, your arms reach toward them to <u>give</u> soothing comfort.

b) You may find that as you gesture *to reject*, your body indicates movement angling away from what you are <u>receiving</u>.

c) If you attempt *to fight*, do you angle your body toward the focus of your fight and <u>give</u> your opponent the sense that you are impenetrable?

d) If you want *to admire* a person, you might lean your head back, and open your posture toward them, <u>receiving</u> them into your world.

Can you see how most tactics, or at least a primary aspect of most tactics, can fit into one of the six Postural Attitudes listed? Do you also see that by translating these Action Tactics into Postural Attitudes that this process will help you translate an intellectual choice of a tactical word right into a physical action?

If you place your Action Tactics in these categories, when you are in rehearsal or working on your script analysis, you can ask yourself, "Does my character want to give, receive, or reflect in this moment?" and then, "What quality of giving, receiving, or reflecting is my character needing: A or B?" Once you answer these two questions you can select an Action Tactic from the Postural Attitude categories to help you refine the choice.

Try This:

Rehearse a scene with your scene partner in which you apply a Postural Attitude to each of the beats. As you rehearse the scene, be as literal as you can with your movement as you apply these general Postural Attitudes.

For example, if you choose to Give 1A in a beat, then literally reach out and physically pull in and embrace and cuddle with your partner during the entire beat. If your next beat is to Reflect 3B, then shift your physical relationship with your partner and fold inward and downward throughout the beat. You will find that applying these broad actions to the scene in this manner will bring the scene to an absurd physical level, feeling as if you are playing, not acting. However, you might also discover entirely new ways to relate to your scene partner physically by applying these actions in such a big way.

As you proceed with your scene work, gradually diminish the larger actions of Giving 1A and Reflecting 3B. Do this until you retain small gestures and movements like reaching out a hand where you used to fully embrace, or slumping down and looking up at your scene partner where you used to actually sink to the floor.

You also might notice that your blocking, tone of voice, and choice of activities during the scene have been influenced by this exercise. With this process, these are logical choices based on your character's tactics, rather than randomly chosen movements simply to provide blocking for the scene.

Action Tactics Categorized By Postural Attitudes

To help you recognize the relationship between Action Tactics and Emotion Tactics, I have categorized lists of Action Tactics under terms that I feel represent the posture and movement elements within the six basic Postural Attitudes of Alba Emoting. These Postural Attitude terms, specific to TEAM for Actors, reflect the shared elements of the Alba Emoting patterns.

A list follows of recommended Action Tactics. These words are broken down into the six Postural Attitudes mentioned previously. Notice that, unlike the words for objectives, these words do not need to imply an ending point. An Action Tactic is used only for the amount of time it remains effective, until it becomes useless or has served its purpose. This is by no means a complete list of possible Action Words. Feel free to add more as you build your own action word vocabulary.

Giving 1A

Assure	Encourage	Prolong
Calm	Entice	Protect
Capture	Flatter	Recommend
Cling	Guard	Reinforce
Comfort	Harbor	Release
Compliment	Hearten	Retain
Contain	Keep	Share
Control	Lend	Shield
Convey	Level	Soothe
Counsel	Linger	Spoil
Cover	Maintain	Support
Defend	Nurture	Suppress
Disclose	Please	Sustain
Divulge	Preserve	Urge
Empower	Prevent	

Giving 1B

Accuse	Experiment	Press
Advise	Face Up To	Probe
Argue	Fight	Provoke
Assault	Figure	Pry
Assure	Find	Pursue
Badger	Follow Force	Push
Belittle	Guarantee	Quiz
Bombard	Harass	Remind
Bully	Hunt	Scar
Chase	Impose	Scorn
Confront	Interrogate	Scrutinize
Corner	Interview	Search
Declare	Intimidate	Shove
Delve	Investigate	Snoop
Demand	Lead	Study
Demoralize	Learn	Terrorize
Derail	Manage	Threaten
Destroy	Needle	Tolerate
Dissect	Oppose	Trap
Eliminate	Penetrate	Undermine
Enforce	Pester	

Receiving 2A

Absorb	Fascinate	Receive
Arouse	Get	Reveal
Assume	Grasp	Revel
Attract	Grope	Seduce
Bait	Hustle	Seize
Charm	Induce	Show
Coax	Inflame	Soak In
Con	Invite	Stimulate
Dazzle	Lure	Swindle
Devour	Lust After	Take
Enchant	Obtain	Tantalize
Expose	Persuade	Tempt

Actions

Receiving 2B

Avoid	Dodge	Recoil
Bluff	Duck	Refuse
Confuse	Elude	Reject
Cower	Escape	Release
Deceive	Evade	Resist
Decline	Fake	Retreat
Deny	Flee	Seclude
Discharge	Free	Skirt
Discount	Hide	Snub
Discover	Ignore	Stop
Dismiss	Leave	Veil
Disregard	Pretend	Withdraw

Reflecting 3A

Bolster	Excite	Mock
Brighten	Flatter	Motivate
Cajole	Fulfill	Please
Captivate	Gratify	Praise
Celebrate	Humor	Rejoice
Cheer	Improve	Relish
Compliment	Indulge	Ridicule
Discover	Ingratiate	Rouse
Enchant	Inspire	Scorn
Encourage	Joke	Tease
Enjoy	Kid	Toy With

Reflecting 3B

Abide	Apologize	Bow
Accept	Appeal	Complain
Acknowledge	Bear	Consent
Admit	Beg	Dampen
Agree	Bend	Deject
Allow	Beseech	Discourage

Reflecting 3B *(continued)*

Disparage	Implore	Resolve
Dissuade	Oblige	Retire
Duck	Permit	Satisfy
Endure	Plead	Settle
Entreat	Request	Understand
Humble		

Try This:

Practice embodying some of these Action Tactics. Are you able to feel commonalities in posture, gestures, and movements with words in the same category? If a word feels different than others, can you get a sense of another Postural Attitude mixing in? If so, which posture do you sense is present, and how is it manifesting in your body? Does it adjust the stance, movement of arms, or facial expression?

Expand on the categorized lists of Postural Attitudes provided. Look through a thesaurus or dictionary and see if you can create more Action Tactics that fit into the six categories. Check these choices against the descriptions and illustrations of the Postural Attitudes provided in this chapter along with the Guidelines for Choosing Action Tactics.

[Example] Postural Attitudes Connected to Action Tactics

Let's go back and look at the Open Scene that has been building throughout the book. Notice that the Action Tactics listed in each beat come from the Postural Attitude categories provided previously.

Actions

Lines	Shift Subtext	Action Tactic & Postural Attitude	
A: Hi. B: Hello.	"I haven't seen you in awhile!"	to lure	2A
A: Great outfit. B: Thanks.	"That jacket would fit me perfectly."	to flatter	3A
A: Where did you get it? B: It's my own.	"Is this a rental?"	to delve	1B
A: Your own? B: Yes. Mine. A: Wow! B: Thanks. A: I mean it. B: Well – again, thanks.	"Perfect for lending!"	to bolster	3A
A: So? I was wondering… B: Wondering? A: If you could…	"Let's get this awkward request over with."	to entreat	3B
B: Really? A: Do you mind?	"Don't make me beg in front my date!"	to plead	3B
B: No. A: No? …. Or No?	"You don't really mean – No."	to coax	2A
B: No. A: All right then. B: Ok.	"What a selfish bastard!"	to recoil	2B

Notice how each beat scoring goes from the general to the specific as you move across the score sheet line from right to left. The Postural Attitude on the far right starts you off with a general idea of what your character is trying to do. Once you select an Action Tactic from the category of Postural Attitudes you start to get more specific with your character's intentions in the beat. The Shift Subtext informs you more about the truth of what the character is thinking while using the Action Tactic in play. Of course, the lines provided by the script identify what the character is actually saying, but it's everything to the right of the scripted lines that provide what you believe your character is actually thinking and doing.

Outside-In or Inside-Out

As you learn to score your scenes, you will find a process that works best for you. You might like to work "from the outside to the inside" and to apply Postural Attitudes that eventually reveal tactics and uncover the character's thoughts. Or you may prefer to work "from the inside to the outside" and approach the text analytically first. The inside-out process first considers your character's thinking process and eventually finds how these thoughts affect actions, tactics, and Postural Attitudes. No specific order in finding these choices is recommended. Simply make clear, strong active choices in support of the character and the given circumstances of the script. If working with a director, check that your choices support the directions and vision of the director.

> ### Try This:
>
> Working from two different scenarios and objectives for the Open Scene, build a scene score for each, by placing columns from left to right that identify Beats, Shift Subtexts, Action Tactics, and Postural Attitudes.
>
> Use two different approaches to create the scene scores. Approach one scene by identifying the Postural Attitudes first and moving toward the left as you fill in the information in each beat. Then, with the other version of the scene, approach the process of

scoring by starting with the Shift Subtexts first and then working toward the right, filling in Postural Attitudes last.

Which process worked best for you? Rehearse the scenes and test your choices. Did one process feel easier to you and produce better results? If so, it could be due to the different order of scoring the scene. In this case, you are recognizing your preferred process, or a development method that better fits the situation.

Dynamic Choices and the Third Choice Theory

In a dynamic performance, an actor translates the common into the uncommon by making acting choices that are strong yet unique, unpredictable, and fresh. Consider a common saying like, "I love you." At first glance, you might want to apply a 2A Action Tactic like *attract* or *enchant* for this sentence. That makes sense, and yet, if you explore other modes of delivering this line, even within the same Postural Attitude category, you will find some intriguing variations on the delivery.

[**Example**] List three different tactics from the 2A category, like *soak in*, *revel*, and *lure*. Say the sentence "I love you" out loud, applying each Action Tactic to the physical, emotional, and vocal delivery of the line. Which sounds most intriguing and fresh to you?

We often select the most obvious choice first, perhaps by looking at the literal meaning of the line and seeing only one delivery option. When you investigate other choices that were not initially considered, you end up with much more creative and unique actions.

The *Third Choice Theory* is a term I have coined and used for the TEAM approach as a way to encourage actors to search for more options. Third Choice Theory can be applied to any inventive or critical thinking activity to find less obvious solutions. The Third Choice Theory implies that your first choice is obvious, your second choice is getting closer to something interesting, and by stretching your imagination a little further, the third choice will often be unique or unexpected. Keep in mind—you don't need to apply this Third Choice Theory to all your tactics, but it is a great tool to use when you want to throw in an unexpected choice or provide a unique spin on the situation, ultimately providing more conflict and surprise.

Try This:

The Third Choice Theory can be practiced with any real life choice, so you can see how it affects a situation. For example, when you enter a room and decide you are going to sit down, consider what your first choice would be; then stop and consider a second seating option. Where would that second option place you in the room, and how would you feel about it? How would this option change your interaction with other people who might be there? Then, stretch your imagination a little bit and pick a third choice—something quite different than from the first two choices. Where did you end up? What perspective did it give you? How did this third choice affect how you related to the room and anyone else in the room?

Then consider the Third Choice Theory for a few other common actions in your life and see what the results are. Consider a third choice for driving home from work, making dinner, rearranging a room, telling a story about an experience, changing your morning routine, etc. What happens when you apply this theory to these everyday actions? Can you see how this would affect actions in a play or movie?

Selecting Tactics Using Antithetical Thinking

Let's also look at Antithetical Thinking or the use of opposites. Referring back to the line, "I love you," we assumed at first we would approach the line with a tactic from the 2A category. The Postural Attitudes and the Basic Emotion categories are set up with clear opposites, and so it is easy to determine opposite actions and reactions for experimentation. Try saying, "I love you" using three different tactics in the 2B category, like *avoid*, *deceive*, and *recoil*. By expressing this line with these opposite tactics, you will find all kinds of new subtexts and layers to the line. When we deliver text in a way that is unusual, another layer is added to text and character interpretation, and we potentially provide an intriguing performance.

> [**Example**] In the movie *Something's Gotta Give*, a scene takes place in a hospital emergency room where the character of Erica Barry, played by Diane Keaton, waits to hear news about the heart attack of her daughter's much older boyfriend, Harry Sandborn, played by Jack Nicholson. A handsome thirty-something ER doctor, played by Keanu Reeves, asks Erica, "You're Mrs. Sandborn?" Erica replies,
>
> "No! Oh, no. No, I'm just...
>
> No, I'm Erica Barry."[32]
>
> With four "No" statements in this sequence of lines, the actor has many line delivery choices to make. When you consider the situation, and particularly the fact that she is not happy at all that her daughter is dating an older man, she can infuse these short "no" lines with a great deal of meaning and intention. Try practicing these lines, imagining the situation. Then—if you get the chance, watch this scene in the film. You might be surprised at how many layers of meaning Diane Keaton is able to find in this short sequence.

Always remember that these choices must still test against the given circumstances and objectives in the script. You are free to make creative choices; just make sure they support the story. As long as they pass that test and don't conflict, you are on the road to making some very dynamic choices.

---

32. "Dailyscript.com," accessed September 1, 2012, Nancy Meyers, *Something's Gotta Give*, (2002), www.dailyscript.com/scripts/SomethingsGottaGive.pdf.

Try This:

Select three beats from one of the open scenes worked on previously in this book, using the Action Tactics assigned to each beat.

(1) Read the segment of the scene out loud with a scene partner, applying the tactics.

(2) Then using Antithetical Thinking, select new tactics from opposite Postural Attitude categories. For example, if a tactic is to entreat from the 3B Postural Attitude, select a tactic from the 3A category.

(3) Read the scene again, applying these new opposite tactics. How was the scene different? How did your partner feel on the receiving end of these tactics?

(4) Go through the process again. This time your scene partner will apply the steps described above, and you will apply the tactics from the first reading. How was the scene different for you on the receiving end of these opposite tactics?

(5) Rehearse the scene again, this time with both of you using the tactics you discovered through Antithetical Thinking. How did the scene feel this time?

(6) Take this exercise one final step further and apply Third Choice Theory to your tactics. Rehearse the scene with your partner and discuss your discoveries. Which choices would you want to keep and why?

[Example] Sample Scene from *The Importance of Being Earnest*

Now, let's apply Action Tactics from the Postural Attitudes to the first four beats of the scene analyzed earlier. Below you will see a replica of the analysis created previously; however, this time a Scene Objective and Victory (see the Thoughts chapter) are applied to guide the process toward selecting Action Tactics. The scene has been placed into a beat shifting grid to help you see clearly where the beat breaks occur, and how choices are applied to the beats.

Scene from *The Importance of Being Ernest*
Algernon's Scene Objective: *to solve the mystery of Ernest's secret identity* (Cognitive)
Victory: He will tell me the truth, the whole truth!

Beat #	Lines from Script	Shift Subtext	Action Tactic	Postural Attitude
1	ALGERNON. My dear fellow, the way you flirt with Gwendolen is perfectly disgraceful. It is almost as bad as the way Gwendolen flirts with you. JACK. I am in love with Gwendolen. I have come up to town expressly to propose to her.	*"Come tell me what you are up to."*	*to lure*	2A
2	ALGERNON. I thought you had come up for pleasure? . . . I call that business. JACK. How utterly unromantic you are! ALGERNON. I really don't see anything romantic in proposing. It is very romantic to be in love. But there is nothing romantic about a definite proposal. Why, one may be accepted. One usually is, I believe. Then the excitement is all over. The very essence of	*"A PROPOSAL?"*	*to dismiss*	2B

Beat #	Lines from Script	Shift Subtext	Action Tactic	Postural Attitude
	romance is uncertainty. If ever I get married, I'll certainly try to forget the fact.			
	JACK. I have no doubt about that, dear Algy. The Divorce Court was specially invented for people whose memories are so curiously constituted.			
	ALGERNON. Oh! There is no use speculating on that subject. Divorces are made in Heaven –			
	[JACK puts out his hand to take a sandwich.			
	ALGERNON at once interferes.]			
3	Please don't touch the cucumber sandwiches. They are ordered specially for Aunt Augusta. [Takes one and eats it.]	*"No cucumber sandwiches for you!"*	*to toy with*	3A
	JACK. Well, you have been eating them all the time.			
	ALGERNON. That is quite a different matter. She is my aunt. [Takes plate from below.] Have some bread and butter. The bread and butter is for Gwendolen. Gwendolen is devoted to bread and butter.			

Beat #	Lines from Script	Shift Subtext	Action Tactic	Postural Attitude
	JACK. [Advancing to table and helping himself.] And very good bread and butter it is too.			
4	ALGERNON. Well, my dear fellow, you need not eat as if you were going to eat it all. You behave as if you were married to her already. You are not married to her already, and I don't think you ever will be.	*"She doesn't really love you."*	*to provoke*	*1B*
	JACK. Why on earth do you say that?			
	ALGERNON. Well, in the first place girls never marry the men they flirt with. Girls don't think it right.			
	JACK. Oh, that is nonsense!			
	ALGERNON. It isn't. It is a great truth. It accounts for the extraordinary number of bachelors that one sees all over the place.			

Read the *Importance of Being Earnest* scene with a scene partner, keeping in mind the Scene Objective. Apply the tactics in your interpretation of the scene. Ask yourself, "How do the tactics lend themselves toward the Scene Objective?"

Change the tactics to entirely different choices, drawing from new categories of Postural Attitudes. Try a few choices using Antithetical Thinking or Third Choice Theory. Then read the scene out loud again. Notice the differences that occur between the scenes simply due to your own changes in tactical choices. Ask your scene partner how he felt on the receiving end of these choices, both times.

Have your scene partner now read Jack's part, applying a Scene Objective and tactics for the first four beats while you simply read Algernon's part and respond to what you receive from your partner. Listen for buttons in Jack's lines and use your reactions to Jack's lines to help you identify Algernon's honest feelings about what Jack is saying. Then determine how Algernon would create a tactical response, after responding to those buttons.

Read the scene again, a fourth time now, and have your partner also apply new tactics from different categories. Discuss the differences in the scenes as well as what it was like to be the one playing the tactics versus the one simply reacting to them.

Actions and Reactions Applied to Activities

Even though this chapter focused on scripted dialogue scenes and interactions with others, all of the lessons provided here can be applied to any physical activity or actor business you may be using in your scene, play, or movie.

[**Example**] If your character has the stage business of cleaning up a room, how many different ways can he clean that room? It depends on how he feels about the task, the reason he is cleaning, and what he is trying to express while he does so. He could be cleaning the room to show his roommate that someone needs to clean this pigpen and to express his disappointment that it has not been done yet. Perhaps he would use a 3B Postural Attitude while he cleans, applying the Action Tactics *accept, tolerate, endure,* and *bear.* To demonstrate the weight of this burden, the actor might adopt a heavy sinking posture as he uses clumsy gestures to pick up and laboriously move furniture, clothing, and debris.

As the roommate fails to acknowledge or help, perhaps the Postural Attitude switches to 1B and he does the cleaning using the tactics *belittle, interrogate,* and *corner.* Then the actor's gestures might have greater muscular control, with more adept movements as he throws objects, tossing them on the floor or sometimes at the roommate.

You can also consider activities that may not be related to what the character says but that provide the character with another mode of expressing his feelings.

[**Example**] Let's look at a different situation, with the same setting and characters, where the character has exciting news and wants to tell his roommate. Throughout the activity of cleaning, the character is looking for the right opportunity to tell his roommate his news, using Action Tactics like *investigate, praise,* and *cajole.* The actor could approach the room-cleaning activity with the 3A Postural Attitude, applying gestures that are light and bouncy as he playfully tosses objects up into the top of the closet, dusts high surfaces, and even lifts things off the floor with agility, verticality, and ease. While doing this, he playfully interacts with his roommate and watches him for the opportunity to bring up the subject that carries the good news.

Try This:

Try doing some basic stage business and activities using the following approaches:

(1) Use different Postural Attitudes and Action Tactics, and see how the activity takes on its own meaning and communicates the character's feelings so much more than words can.

(2) Apply the Third Choice Theory and Antithetical Thinking to explore new ways to conduct the stage business, particularly if it helps reveal the character's subtext.

(3) Assign Subtext Statements, and actually mumble them to yourself as you practice the activity to help you discover Action Tactics and Postural Attitudes that would more clearly reflect how you feel about either the activity or the given circumstances.

Solving Stiffness in An American Daughter

I am directing Wendy Wasserstein's An American Daughter, *an intriguing play about women coping with political life in Washington D.C. The majority of the cast in the play are young college students, attempting to play characters that are intricate and politically savvy doctors, professors, journalists, and nationally respected authors. If the actors don't find ways to physicalize the urgent needs and desires of these very heady characters, this wordy play could fall into the depths of dull, talking-heads theatre.*

I am working with the lead actress playing Lyssa, a newly appointed Surgeon General. The entire action of this very talk-centered play takes place in Lyssa's home in Georgetown. The opening scene mentions that Lyssa is cleaning up after her young boys while also dealing with the news of her appointment and how her friends, family, and the public at large are responding to that news. The actress playing Lyssa is a very talented, honest actor for someone so young; however, she struggles with physicalizing her thoughts and feelings. I notice that when she engages in an activity, greater levels of expressive posture, gestures, and variations of emotional life flow from her, like no other time in her acting.

I decide to give this actress many activities throughout the play and assign Action Tactics to the various beats of these activities. The stage business of cleaning, clearing, and organizing fits perfectly within the given circumstances of the play. It is justified by her frustration with all the people and news media equipment intruding her home environment. In the beginning of the play, her cleaning has more qualities of 3A, as she is filled with the excitement of the new appointment and the great potential for making an impact on the country's health care situation. As the play progresses and the media start to take over her life, manipulating her words and actions, the character of Lyssa feels she is losing control. The straightening and organizing become more intensive, fueled by her need to have control over something. She applies 1B qualities to her actions, and her acting exhibits the physical state of someone desperately trying to retain her dignity and hold onto the life she worked hard to build over the years.

The actors in this play would give me a wry smile occasionally during rehearsals, asking "What am I cleaning or organizing now?" The props crew had a challenge in keeping up with all the objects for these activities. In the end, the actors were grateful to have these priceless extensions of their tactics and feelings. As our audiences sat, almost feeling like they were peeking into the personal lives of these Washington D.C. elites in such a private, personalized setting, they were presented with intricately layered, truthful characters engaged in passionate and physically dedicated pursuits.

Applying an Action Approach

If you would like to use an Action Approach as the MVP for your acting, follow these steps:

1. Read and investigate the entire script for clues to your character's actions, activities, and behaviors.

2. Determine Postural Attitudes for the layers of your character's personality, considering one for each: (1) primary, (2) social mask, and (3) shadow self. Practice embodying these attitudes, putting them into action and gesture in order to build a physical characterization.

3. Break your scenes into beats and assign Action Tactics to each beat.

4. Consider facades and masks, reactions and discoveries, and the button when scoring and rehearsing the scenes. Use third choice theory and antithetical thinking in some areas to go beyond obvious choices.

5. Go over all the checklists for establishing beats and Action Tactics to check your final work.

6. Rehearse your scenes applying Postural Attitudes, Action Tactics, and activities.

7. Invite a Side Coach to watch and remind you of your Postural Attitudes and Action Tactics (see Manifestation Chapter for more information on side coaching).

8. Once the scene is memorized and rehearsed several times with the

Action approach, check to see that aspects of thought and emotion have also clearly manifested in your performance. If not, apply exercises and techniques from those chapters to help bring these elements into your acting work.

Summary Of Actions

Your character's actions and reactions can be constructed consciously through applying a series of basic Postural Attitudes and specific Action Tactics. These choices will influence your character's physical life, personality traits, activities, gestures, blocking, and reactions. You can also provide intricate layers of actions by assigning certain tactics that express your character's social mask or facade, while engaging impulsive reactions to reveal your true feelings and thoughts. Finally, by applying Third Choice Theory and Antithetical Thinking, you have a technique for creating dynamic choices in moments that need a unique spin, intrigue, surprise, or originality.

This chapter introduces the basic tools of scoring and preparing for rehearsals using Action Tactics and Postural Attitudes. As you study and refine physical actions and expression techniques, you will find that your acting reaches greater levels of quality, displays intricate layers of well-rounded characterization, and develops a wide interpretive range, adaptable to any role. You will have, as Chekhov coined, *a wise body*: "What result can come to the actor from such meditative work upon his body as a threefold form? We realize that the body can be either 'wise' or 'stupid' on stage. Neither evening dress nor Greek tunic can hide from the audience the impression the body makes from the stage.[33]

[33] Chekhov, *On the Technique of Acting*, 55.

Further Study

1. *Building a Character*, by Constantine Stanislavski

2. *On the Technique of Acting*, by Michael Chekhov

3. "Alba Emoting: A Psychophysiological Technique to Help Actors Create and Control Real Emotions," Theatre Topics, 9/93, Vol.3, Num.2, by Susana Bloch

"When the actor in his creativeness

measures up to a remarkable text, the words

of his part prove...the easiest form of verbal

embodiment with which he can make

manifest his own creative emotions

through his inner score." [34]

— Constantine Stanislavski

Chapter 5

Manifestation

Manifest *(verb): to make clear or evident to the eye or to the understanding; show plainly. Latin origin,* manifestus *and* manifestare*: to make public, detected in the act, evident, visible. Synonyms: reveal, demonstrate, and express.*[35]

Manifestation can mean the indication of existence, the presence of something, a public display, or clear appearance or understanding of something. A manifesto is "a public declaration of principles, policies, or intentions," and a manifestation is the "resulting belief revealed."[36] In the TEAM, manifestation represents how the beliefs and intentions of the character reveal or display themselves through embodied acting. Manifestation techniques take the theoretical to the tangible and believable.

Stanislavski describes this culminating step as the Through Action or the Unbroken Line where the "inner motive forces will be drawn into action."[37] In order to embody this Through Action, an actor must (1) manifest the character's inner and outer story, (2) make understandable and believable connections with the character, and (3) recognize that the character is also striving for a manifested result, or the evidence of achieving a victory.

Here is where the TEAM culminates with techniques that bridge the theories explored in earlier chapters to the actor's understanding and embodiment of

34. Constantine Stanislavski, *Creating a Role* (New York: Theatre Arts Books, 1961), 95.
35. Dictionary.com (2012) http://dictionary.reference.com/
36. "The Online Etymology Dictionary," accessed September 1, 2012, http://www.etymonline.com.
37. Stanislavski, *An Actor Prepares*, 253.

the role. This chapter provides methods for making Personal Connections with the character's objectives and needs. Steps are provided for creating, using, and adjusting a TEAM score in rehearsal and for specific acting occasions. The TEAM for Actors side-coaching process provides a culminating method for encouraging embodiment of the TEAM score and for providing feedback when parts of the TEAM are not clearly revealed in the acting. The chapter then concludes with suggestions for further exploration and study of various embodiment techniques that can be used as companions to the TEAM.

There is a common directive given to actors: "Be believable." When this is not met, a director might say, "I didn't believe you in that moment." As you learn more about Manifestation techniques, consider this: if you fully analyze your character's thoughts, emotions, and actions—but are unable to find some semblance of belief in these discoveries, how can you broadcast a believable situation for your character to the audience? Can you convey truth and belief if you don't actually believe in the situation you are acting?

Inhabiting the Part

To inhabit a part means that you are believing in and expressing the thoughts, actions, and reactions of the character from inside-out. In other words, are living in their words and thoughts. Some characters you will play may be very accessible to you, and then others may require an understanding of challenging life circumstances that appear at first to be out of your reach. Such characters may have experiences so foreign to your own that you may not even be able to imagine, let alone believe. In order to portray these experiences fully and truthfully, you will need to find a way to connect them, or bring them closer, to your own experience.

The Essence of Extreme Loss

When I was thirty years old, I was acting in a world premiere of a new Irish play, At the Black Pig's Dyke. *The play depicts the lives of a mother and daughter living on a small farm in Northern Ireland during the early 1960s, or the beginning of "the troubles." At Christmas time in county Antrim, men dressed as mummers—wearing cloaks and tall cone-shaped masks made out of potato sacks and straw—would visit people's homes to sing holiday songs and play practical jokes. However, with the dispute between Catholics and Protestants, some were using the mummer disguises to intimidate and attack their identified enemies.*

I play the lead role of Lizzie, who is struggling with the murder of her husband by men disguised as mummers. In one particularly long monologue delivered out to the audience, my character tells the story of how she has come home from picking up her daughter at school and cannot find her husband. She takes her young daughter's hand and starts to wander the fields, calling for him. She eventually stumbles upon her husband's dead body, and she and her daughter are faced with the gruesome scene, discovering him "slashed to pieces" and lying in a pool of blood.

While rehearsing this play I found I was able to make solid connections with most of Lizzie's scenes and objectives; however, whenever I came to this monologue I ended up delivering it from an emotional distance, like a storyteller too far removed from the situation. I knew I had to find a way to connect more fully with this woman's true story of incredible loss, fear, and pain. Having no husband or child in my personal life at the time, and never encountering a situation of such extreme loss and brutality, I knew I needed to find a way to connect some essence of this woman's story with my own personal life experiences. But how?

(story continued later in this chapter)

Essential Action

The Essential Action helps actors understand the essence, or basic element, of anything they are attempting to portray. Connecting with a character's Essential Action is much like empathizing with another person's situation, feelings, and motives in real life. It is important for an actor to first empathize with the character before attempting to display this person's needs, desires, and reactions in performance. Once the Essential Action is identified, you can personally understand how to embody the situation through objectives, tactics, actions and emotions. No matter how different the role is from your life experiences or how unique the occasion is, if you identify the essence of that character's situation and then relate it to your own life experience, you will be able obtain a core understanding and empathy for the situation.

Universal Qualities in Essential Actions

In order to identify Essential Actions, you must first understand the use of Universal Qualities. Identifying universal qualities in a person or situation is recognizing what is *of or belonging to all*. This is the first step in achieving empathy for and achieving an understanding of another's life experience. A simple way to identify universal qualities is to ask yourself, "What is the common human action in this situation?"

> [**Example**] Tallulah Bankhead, the famous actress of the 1920s and '30s, once remarked that in order to play a murderer, all she needed to do was remember a time when she picked up a broom, determined to kill a mouse loose in her apartment. Here the actress is referring to the Essential Action, "the intent to kill." Some might think that killing is not a Universal Action that a majority of people could understand. However, if you consider how many people might quickly adopt the action "to kill" when met with a mosquito, fly, or bee invading their space, you may understand that the intent to kill rises very quickly and instinctively in many. Yes—killing another human being is a much bigger and horrific act than killing a mosquito. However, the Essential Action of "the intent to kill" is still present as a common action in both.

Once an Essential Action is identified, you can place it in the given circumstances of the script, and if the stakes of those circumstances are higher (as in the difference between murdering an insect and murdering a person), allow the intensity and gravity of the action to grow and match with its environment.

> [**Example**] I often explain that this act of growing an Essential Action in given circumstances is like those little shrunken sponge toys

found in coin operated vending machines. These sponge toys are tiny capsules, containing a piece of compressed sponge. You are instructed to drop the capsule in a glass of water, and watch the sponge grow into a recognizable shape of an animal or object. In this analogy the shrunken sponge is the Essential Action, and the water is the given circumstances. Once placed in an environment that encourages its expansion, it grows into something recognizable and playable.

The Essence of Extreme Loss (story continued)

After considerable time and contemplation, I realized the basic essence of what Lizzie was experiencing was primarily "witnessing the destruction of something/someone she held very dear." This was a fairly universal experience, particularly if I allowed the event to be the destruction of some<u>thing</u> dear, as well as some<u>one</u>. Once I made this discovery, I asked myself how I have felt in my life when I discovered something dear to me had been destroyed. As I explored this, the basic feelings of shock, grief, anger, and fear emerged from my memories. I pondered further. A person coming upon a scene of destruction would most likely first experience shock at the scene, then grief over the loss. The grief would most likely mix with anger, toward the individual who caused the destruction. Then a sense of fear might also mix in as one realizes the potential ongoing threat, if the person causing the destruction is still around.

Using this process of connecting my own experiences with Lizzie's story made playing her brutal discovery much more attainable. I used the essence of this Universal Action as a way to personally empathize with the situation. I then took this small essence of personal belief and used my imagination to immerse fully in Lizzie's given circumstance. Soon it all became very real to me.

That night at rehearsal, when I approached the monologue and applied this actor homework to my performance, the director was thrilled, and she asked, "Can you duplicate that? Please don't tell me it was a brief moment of inspiration, never to return again!" I could duplicate it because I had a process I could rely on and a clear understanding of what I had found in order to fully connect with this story.

Try This:

Below are some examples of Essential Actions. See if you recall a life experience that would qualify as a match to each of these actions. If you can, do you also feel that most others could as well? If so, the actions have universal qualities, and would be good choices for Essential Actions.

Examples of Essential Actions

to achieve something that is commendable

to participate in something dangerous

to acquire something of great value

to recognize I am in an awkward situation

to flirt with another to gain access

to witness someone receiving punishment

to pretend I am someone else

to believe that a group can be trustworthy

to know I am capable of completing a difficult task

to experience someone's downfall

Wording Essential Action Statements

Much like the wording of the Objective Statement covered in the Thoughts chapter, the wording of the Essential Action statement must be crafted carefully so that you have a clear communication of the core idea presented. Using a different verb, adverb, adjective, or noun will change the entire meaning of the Essential Action. It is the same as giving someone directions to a place and telling them to turn left instead of right at an intersection. They will end up in the wrong place.

[Examples]

Consider the Essential Action *to experience someone's downfall.*

Notice how the meaning of this Essential Action changes with different **verb** choices:

> *to watch someone's downfall*
>
> *to orchestrate someone's downfall*
>
> *to investigate someone's downfall*

The use of *to watch* implies some distance, *to orchestrate* states the individual caused the downfall, and *to investigate* suggests the individual is removed from the event and is engaged in a problem-solving action. The initial use of *to experience* suggests it is also affecting the individual, with some personal loss involved.

[Examples]

Now consider minor changes in the final **noun**, "downfall":

> *to experience someone's destruction*
>
> *to experience someone's failure*
>
> *to experience someone's loss*

The use of *destruction* implies an outside force causing the result, *failure* suggests that the resulting condition was caused largely by the individual, and *loss* could introduce a multitude of personal losses outside of the individual, like possessions or loved ones. The initial use of *downfall* suggests that the individual was in a place of high status and, due to various factors, fell from that position.

Essential Action Statement Guidelines

Here are some guidelines to remember when creating an Essential Action statement for an objective or situation:

(1) Retain the intent of the Action Word used in the Objective Statement, by either using the same word or a similar one.

(2) Replace specific character, place, or thing names with indefinite pronouns.

(3) Maintain the qualities of the adverbs and adjectives used in the original objective.

(4) Verify that the situation describes the core essence of the original objective.

(5) Ask yourself, "Is this a universal situation that is common to most people?"

[Examples]

In the examples listed below, the numbers in parentheses match the Essential Action Statement Guidelines.

Objective: To charm my co-worker into taking my place at an important meeting
Essential Action: (1) to charm (2) someone into doing (3) an important favor (4 & 5)

Objective: to acquire the prestigious position of company president
Essential Action: (1) to acquire (2) something (3) prestigious (4 & 5)

Objective: to conspire with my sister on a solid plan for winning back our home
Essential Action: (1) to conspire with (2) another to gain (3) a valuable possession (4 & 5)

Objective: to construct the greenhouse without my father's help
Essential Action: (1) to build (2) something (3) challenging on my own (4 & 5)

Essential Actions for Situations

If you are using Essential Action to help you understand a brief challenging situation within a scene, remember that it is possible to assign objectives to beats in a scene as well. In such cases, write a beat objective, following the same guidelines used for Objective Statements. The only difference is that you can also use short-term, Action-Tactic words as described in the Actions chapter.

[Examples]

Possible Situation: A bride dressing for her wedding ceremony
Essential Action: to prepare myself for an important event

Possible Situation: A character seeing a ghost
Essential Action: to witness something beyond my comprehension

Possible Situation: A person masquerading as a missionary in a
poor village
Essential Action: to pretend I am behind a worthy cause

Possible Situation: The spouse of a president who is impeached
Essential Action: to experience someone's downfall

Possible Situation: A fisherman stranded at sea in a motorboat
that won't start
Essential Action: to challenge myself with a difficult task

Exercise
Rewording Objectives into Essential Action Statements

Look at these objectives from plays and movies mentioned previously within this text. See if you can identify the Universal Action of each objective and write an Essential Action Statement for each. The first three are completed as examples.

1. Objective: **To prove to my friends that this painting is a valued piece of art**
Universal Action: <u>to prove</u>
Essential Action Statement: <u>To prove the value of something to disbelievers</u>

2. Objective: **To verify that God is my baby's father**
Universal Action: <u>to verify</u>
Essential Action Statement: <u>To verify something beyond the comprehension of another</u>

3. Objective: **To win the race with honor**
Universal Action: <u>to win</u>
Essential Action Statement: <u>To win something by using honorable conduct</u>

4. Objective: **To protect my young witness from the murderers**
Universal Action: _____
Essential Action Statement:_____

_____

5. Objective: **To discover groundbreaking research left by my mentor**
Universal Action: _____
Essential Action Statement:_____

_____

6. Objective: **To teach her that all things in life are based in numbers**
Universal Action: _____
Essential Action Statement:_____

_____

7. Objective: **To create a provocatively daring thesis project**
Universal Action: _____
Essential Action Statement:_____

_____

8. Objective: **To empower my troops to make history by winning the battle**
Universal Action: _____
Essential Action Statement:_____

_____

Try This:

Practice identifying objectives along with their Universal Qualities and Essential Actions in short stories, folk tales, short plays, and scenes from other fiction and non-fiction. The more you challenge your ability to identify the Universal Actions in all forms of dramatic literature, the better you will become at quickly identifying these elements within scripted roles and acting situations.

Exercise
Assigning Essential Actions to Challenging Situations

Essential Action statements can also help you connect with extremely challenging situations your character may be experiencing. Imagine the situations listed in this exercise are experiences you must portray in your acting. Identify the Universal Action. Then write an Essential Action Statement. The first three are completed as examples.

1. Situation: **committing suicide**
Universal Action: to abandon
Essential Action Statement: Abandoning a situation that is beyond my coping abilities

2. Situation: **trapped in a mine**
Universal Action: <u>to be trapped</u>
Essential Action Statement: <u>Trapped in something with limited time and means for escape</u>

3. Situation: **getting married**
Universal Action: <u>to commit</u>
Essential Action Statement: <u>Committing to something with long-term expectations</u>

4. Situation: **receiving a big reward**
Universal Action: _____
Essential Action Statement:_____

_____

5. Situation: **mortally wounded**
Universal Action: _____
Essential Action Statement:_____

_____

6. Situation: **lost at sea**
Universal Action: _____
Essential Action Statement:_____

_____

7. Situation: **given a big promotion**
Universal Action: _____
Essential Action Statement:_____

_____

8. Situation: **giving birth**

Universal Action: _____

Essential Action Statement:_____

_____

9. Situation: **face to face with an enemy**

Universal Action: _____

Essential Action Statement:_____

_____

10. Situation: **alone in a house being burgled**

Universal Action: _____

Essential Action Statement:_____

_____

Did you struggle with identifying the Universal Action and Essential Action Statements for some of these situations? These examples were chosen because they are very challenging and may take some time and discussion to discover the universal qualities an actor can connect with in order to truthfully play each situation.

Try This:

Create a list of challenging situations beyond the list provided in the exercise. Identify the Universal Action and Essential Action Statement for each. With practice, identifying Universal Actions and Essential Action Statements for challenging situations will become much easier and make empathizing with any character or situation in the future much more approachable.

Professional Actor Faced with a Challenging Role

I am directing Paula Vogel's How I Learned to Drive *for a professional theatre company. The play depicts the life of a young girl, nicknamed Li'l Bit, from her early childhood through her eighteenth birthday. The focus of the play is to gradually reveal her unorthodox relationship with her uncle, nicknamed Uncle Peck. Uncle Peck has an unusual fascination with his niece. He spends a lot of time alone with her, and he suggests that they engage in activities where Li'l Bit is modeling for pictures or where he has the opportunity to have physical contact with her, as when he encourages her to sit on his lap in the car. As Li'l Bit grows up and gets closer to her eighteenth birthday, Uncle Peck clearly has his sights set on taking Li'l Bit to a hotel for a weekend to "celebrate" her coming of age. He sends her notes, buys her presents, and admits that he has always loved her in a special way.*

The actor playing Uncle Peck has been a professional actor for years. As we begin our early rehearsals and discussions of roles, I see that he is clearly struggling with connecting to the motives and needs of Uncle Peck. The actor requests a meeting with me outside of rehearsal to talk about our perceptions of Uncle Peck's life and back story. What is his relationship with his wife, Aunt Mary? What was his childhood like? Did any adults in his childhood have inappropriate relationships with him, which formed this adult behavior? The back story we create forms a clear picture and foundation for the personality and behavior of Uncle Peck.

We agree that it is important for the balance of the play's action to depict Uncle Peck with sincerity, and not to portray him as evil or predatory. We agree he is feeling confused and personally tortured by his own sincere desires and affection for Li'l Bit but is driven by his true love for her and believes that if his love feels pure, he is hurting her. I see that our discussion of Uncle Peck is helping the actor find clear, intellectual connections with Uncle Peck, but we are still talking about him from a place of distance. The next and most challenging step is for the actor to personally connect with these motives and feelings.

Manifestation

Finally, I ask him, "How can you connect with Uncle Peck's needs and motivations to fondle and molest his young niece?" The actor recoils with disgust, "I can't! That is the problem. I think he is sick, and I sit in judgment of him every time I try to play him."

I gently pursue the subject with him: "Let's look at what Uncle Peck does not have in his life with Aunt Mary and other adults. Now, without focusing on the act of molesting, or the fact that she is underage, what does he gain by having a close relationship with Li'l Bit that he does not get from adults?" The benefits immediately pour out of the actor's mouth: innocence, uncomplicated communications, adoration, respect, and a fresh start or new chapter to look forward to. We agree that these are all Universal Actions, and easy to empathize with. I ask the actor, "Can you focus on these needs in your scenes with Li'l Bit and see her through this lens? Can you look at the actress playing Li'l Bit as an innocent, uncomplicated, and fresh answer to your need to escape your tortured life?" The actor nods in agreement.

I then ask, "Have you had times in your life where you were trying to get something you wanted but lacked the appropriate means to get it? And perhaps you were frustrated with yourself because you knew you were not using the right methods but kept trying anyway because your desire was so strong?" The actor nods again and offers, "Oh—yes, well, do you mean like bad answers to interview questions? Or getting in a fight with a loved one and saying all the wrong things, even though I am trying to apologize and make it right again?" I let him know he is on the right track and add, "Can you also recognize that Uncle Peck is essentially in a similar situation? He wants to form an affectionate relationship with Li'l Bit, but he is not using the right methods. His motives are coming from a sincere place in his own perspective, but his impulsive actions are unacceptable in the eyes of others, and he knows it. And so, he is personally tortured afterwards, but in the moment, he is impulsively using the actions available in his limited and skewed list of tactics." The actor playing Uncle Peck sighs with relief "Now that is something I can understand, and play!"

207

The Essential Action Bridges Two Worlds

Look at this image of two large hills separated by a deep cavern. Imagine that the hill on the right represents your character's life and experience. Sitting at the top of that hill is your character's current objective or situation. Then imagine the hill on the left represents your life experience. There appears to be a great divide between these two hills, and these two lives.

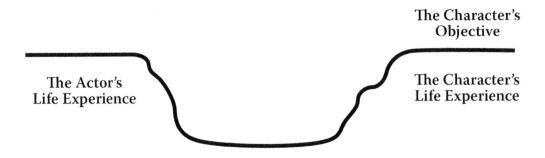

At first it may appear as if there is no way you can connect the two. Then, imagine that the Essential Action is the bridge that connects the two separate worlds. Your Life Experience Hill holds the potential to bridge the gap by accessing common experiences between you and your character. The first step in building this bridge is to identify the universal essence of your character's objective or situation. The next step is to connect your own life experiences with that universal essence so you can cross over the bridge.

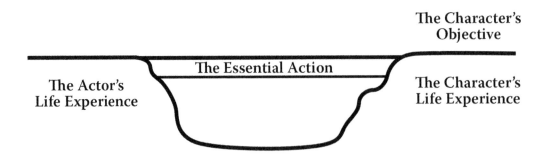

Empathy Approached through Personal Connections

I have created the term, Personal Connections, to capture the essence of all the techniques used for bridging the actor's life experiences with that of the character's. Making personal life connections with characters and situations was first described by Stanislavski in Creating a Role, using the terms As If and the Magic If.[38] He encouraged actors to "feel oneself in the part" in order to truly connect with the life and experiences of the character. Sigmund Freud also used an As If theory in *Future of An Illusion* in order to explain how a person can empathize with the unknowns.[39] Many acting teachers since then have utilized methods for making personal life connections by applying Imaginary Circumstances, Emotional Substitution, Affective Memory, and Sense Memory methods. Although each of these terms stem from specific acting school theories, all of these are a form of achieving empathy with the character's circumstances.

It is a natural human process for a person to imagine how she might behave if she were in a situation she has never yet personally experienced. How often have you tried to understand the motivations and feelings of another person? Can you remember times when you tried to empathize with another by recalling a similar personal experience from your own life and imagining yourself "in the shoes" of that person? Can you recall a time when you felt challenged to understand someone else's motivations, and through this need to empathize, your mind searched for common ground? You most likely identified the Essential Action of the situation and achieved some level of empathy for the other person by connecting that universal life experience to something you had in common. This is the basic process of applying Essential Action and Personal Connections to what first appears as unknown or beyond your understanding. The Personal Connection is similar to the common saying, "Put yourself in the other person's place, as if it happened to you." You are making the effort to empathize with the experiences of another by inviting an imagined participation in their story.

Using Personal Connections to Cross the Essential Action Bridge

Applying the Personal Connection to an acting role is the act of combining small aspects of your life experience with imagination and empathy in order to live

---

38. Stanislavski, *Creating a Role*, 213-233.
39. Sigmund Freud, *Future of An Illusion* (New York: Classic House Books, 2009), 30.

vicariously through the character's experiences. Sometimes you will need to play roles that have life experiences far beyond your own, which possibly appear out of reach for your imagination. Using the Personal Connection along with the Essential Action is a means to cross over the bridge into the world of your character.

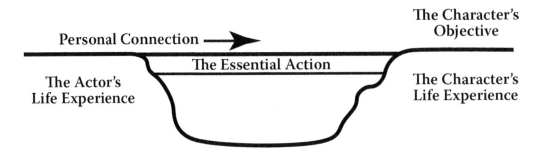

Keep in mind that we do this naturally and automatically when we listen to someone tell a story about a dramatic or extraordinary event that occurred to them. As we listen, our thoughts search for common ground, and we might even say, "I can only imagine" or "I know what you mean." We might then launch into telling our own experience of what we feel is a similar event in our lives. If there is a group of people listening to an extraordinary story, this automatic empathetic process can be a natural way to start conversation, as they search for common ground and look for ways to connect with each other. They are identifying the Essential Action of someone else's story, and then telling their own version of a similar experience, or sharing their Personal Connection.

[**Example**] Here is a possible string of stories that could stem from this process of identifying Essential Actions and Personal Connections.

Someone in a group may start with a story of how he was enduring a 17-hour ride on a train in Italy, which was so full he and his friends had to pack into the hallways between the individual seating cars. With the long train ride ahead and desperately in need of sleep, they opted to sit or lie down on the hallway floor, resigning themselves to a dirty floor and being stepped over by those headed for the bathroom.

Then someone else shares a story of how she was traveling as a tourist in Guatemala and ended up taking a bus that quickly became packed with people and crates of chickens and exotic birds. The bus ride was long and hot, with no air conditioning. They were expected to accommodate all who needed a ride, and eventually she ended up sitting on her friend's lap for the rest of the trip. The stench of overheated bodies, animals, and unusually strong-smelling food that people started eating during the ride was too much for her. She sat on her friend's lap by the window and rode the entire trip with her head out the window as the bus snaked through the rolling hills.

Essential Action she identified within the first story: *Forgoing normal social behaviors to survive a difficult environment*

The string of essential stories continues as another person offers his experience of riding in a hot, packed subway in New York City when the electricity went out in the tunnels and the subway stopped suddenly in the dark, hot tunnels of the underground. He was on his way home from work, exhausted from a long, stressful day. He sat sweating in his good work clothes for hours until they finally restored the power to the trains.

Essential Action he identified within the second story: *Enduring uncomfortable conditions in an unexpected location*

Notice how each storyteller subconsciously found the Essential Action within the previous story. If the story chain were to continue, down the line the subject of the stories might morph into an entirely new topic as each person identifies one aspect of the previous story to which they felt some kinship. All of the resulting stories, after the very first offering, are the individual's Personal Connection to an Essential Action identified in the previous story.

Try This:

Imagine you were in a social situation in which the story string, described previously, was shared. How might you relate to the last story in the string? What Essential Action do you identify with that third story? What story might you then contribute as you identify a Personal Connection from your own life?

Personal Connections with the Final Goodbye in Our Town

I am working as an emotion coach with the actress who plays Emily in a production of Our Town. *She is struggling with making connections with Emily's final monologue of the play, often called the "Goodbye Monologue." Emily died giving birth to a child and has joined the many souls who have passed away, those she knew when she was living in her small town. She asks for one last glimpse of her life and returns to her past to relive a morning in her childhood. As she visits this scene, she finds it is too disappointing when she realizes that the living are so focused on the day-to-day activities that they don't really take the time to look at each other and appreciate what they have. Emily's last moments in the monologue involve looking back at her life and saying goodbye to the simple pleasures of life, like sunflowers, food, coffee, ironed dresses, hot baths, sleeping, and waking up.*

The student portraying Emily is a delightfully passionate young actress who has taken the initiative to seek personal coaching from me on this moment. Having never worked with her before, I quickly find that she takes direction very well but that this particular moment in the play is elusive to her. As a starting point in our work, I ask her to show me what she has so far. She proceeds to deliver the monologue from a place of distance, as if commenting on Emily's situation from a narrative perspective rather than actually feeling this transformation of leaving the simple pleasures in life, never to experience them again. I learn that her director wants her to really feel and express the shock of her discoveries, and then the grief of loss, and finally achieve a brief moment of peaceful acceptance.

I work with the actress using some Alba Emoting techniques to help her access these emotions, and I find that by helping her connect physically to grief, essentially living in her words, and not commenting on them, it allows her to let go of this distancing narrative quality. We practice a section of the monologue a couple times, giving her permission to fully connect with the physical qualities of grief (3B), and not worry about "performing" the monologue, which often translates to actors as "narrating from a distance." She immediately finds the weighty physical qualities of grief, sadness, and loss.

We recognize that her director does not want a delivery with this level of fully exposed grief. The director desires the grief to be "just under the surface," emerging only when she mentions things that overwhelm her ability to explain, becoming a brief moment of raw unprotected feeling that cannot be denied.

I ask her to run the monologue again, and this time to allow the grief to rise up when she is listing some things that make her sad to leave behind. I ask her to consider the list of items she will never experience again and make Personal Connections of meaning with them. As she performs the monologue again I quietly reinforce the idea of this goodbye by occasionally calling out, "Never again!" as she mentions each item. In the middle of the list, where she says, "And food and coffee," the actress suddenly gulps and tears emerge as she works through the rest of the list, truly grieving over the idea of "never again." She fully embodies this grief for a very brief, exposed moment.

As the monologue approaches conclusion, she works to recover her composure. She turns away from the scene that represents her past, and looks up at the stage lights with peaceful acceptance (2A). Soft tears still dampen her cheeks as she expresses with awe, "Oh, earth, you are too wonderful for anybody to realize you."

The actress has made a break-through that allows her to truly feel this transformation. She is delighted with this discovery, and as we talk afterwards about her findings, I ask her if she wants to share with me what helped her make the pivotal shift into grieving the goodbye list. She smiles at me and reveals, "I know it sounds silly, but I LOVE coffee, and as I said goodbye to coffee and heard you say, 'Never again,' I could not imagine never having another cup of coffee again. As I made that connection to my own life, I found my words immediately catch in my throat and the tears welled, and I was there!"

Important Note Concerning the Use of Personal Connection Experiences

The Personal Connection approach to empathizing with your character or situation is meant as actor homework in preparation for rehearsal or to be used as a rehearsal exercise. It is used as a means to recall how it felt to experience an essentially similar situation or gain a closer perspective on an elusive idea or concept. You would then use this connection to collect additional information on emotions felt and actions taken at the time and to apply those to the imaginary given circumstances within the performance. It is not recommended to use these exact life situations in the midst of performances. It could potentially take you out of the imaginary world you are playing. Using the actual Personal Connection during a performance could immerse you into your own past too deeply and disconnect you from actively engaging and interacting with the actors and situations present in the performance moment.

Another consideration for selecting Personal Connections is to make sure the event you choose is not a situation that is a very recent, unresolved, or traumatic one. Very recent situations do not have the benefit of analytic distance. Emotionally unresolved situations might still retain heavily entangled emotions and cause deep traumatic effects on an individual recalling them. Traumatic Personal Connections are not beneficial to you as an acting tool, nor are they healthy for you to recall and work through while trying to prepare a role for performance. Remember the reference made earlier in this chapter where Tallulah Bankhead said that in order to play a murderer, all she needed to do was remember a time when she picked up a broom, determined to kill a mouse loose in her apartment. She is referring to a Personal Connection with the Essential Action, *to kill*. Likewise, if you are playing a role where you need to empathize with a character who is dealing with the death of a loved one, it is not recommended to use a traumatic and unresolved personal loss of a loved one in your history. If you simply connect with the Essential Action, *to lose something very dear to me*, you can use any number of personal situations that contain similar emotions and actions, but are not personally traumatic or unresolved.

Examples of Personal Connections to Essential Actions

Referring back to my story of playing the role of Lizzie in the Irish drama *At the Black Pig's Dyke*, I identified the essence of my character's situation, *to witness the destruction of someone very dear.* Even though I had a personal experience where my dog was run over by a car, I chose not to use it because it was still, even after twenty years, an unresolved emotional experience. Since I felt that the *someone* aspect of the essence might place me in a Personal Connection that had the potential of being far too traumatic for me as an acting tool, I changed the indirect pronoun to *something.* I then created a Personal Connection for the situation that helped me bridge the gap between her life and my own.

It took me quite some time to find something from my own thirty years of living a relatively safe and peaceful life that would bridge the gap between Lizzie's situation and my own life experience. I made a list of "things that are very dear to me" and added "where I witnessed their destruction." The resulting Personal Connection found was, "When I witnessed the destruction of my new car." In this experience I was driving my first new car, purchased just one month earlier, going to work at my first full-time position at a college. The new car represented stability, success, and freedom after years of old cars breaking down and leaving me stranded on road-sides. The car was indeed very dear to me.

One winter day, while I was driving through a fairly vacant campus during winter break, a young man in a large SUV stopped at a stop sign in front of me and suddenly and very quickly backed up. Even though I slammed on the horn as I desperately tried to put my car in reverse, within seconds his car smashed into the hood of my new car, creating an accordion fold of new car metal before my very eyes. (I later learned that he intended to turn around in the middle of this "vacant street," and did not see my smaller car behind him nor hear my horn because he was playing very loud music.)

During this event, I felt the emotions of shock, fear, loss, anger, self-protection, and disbelief. I also found that in the months to follow, my body would automatically tense each time I pulled up behind another, larger car at an intersection or stop sign, as my muscle memory instinctively reconnected to the accident. I imagined that these would be core emotions and physical reactions one might feel in Lizzie's situation and that they could affect her interactions with others well after the event. Although these identified emotions and physical behaviors needed to be heightened to reach the extreme circumstance she was experiencing, they provided a clear bridge to the essence of Lizzie's situation.

I also identified the Essential Action of Lizzie's Scene Objective as, *to protect an innocent from harm.* The Personal Connection for this Essential Action was much easier for me to find. Growing up in the middle of five children, and having spent much of my life working with children or animals, protecting an innocent held many life experiences for me. With this in mind, my Personal Connection could be, "When I was protecting my little brother from the bullies on our block." This event took place when I was much younger, and involved gathering my friends to walk my brother home, protecting him from being out-numbered. This event was far enough in the past to provide analytic distance and was not an emotionally unresolved situation for me.

To provide another example of how an actor uses Personal Connections to cross into the world of the character, the actor playing Uncle Peck in *How I Learned to Drive* identified the essence of Uncle Peck's objective throughout the play as, *to pursue something highly desirous but by using poor methods.* In order to help the actor connect with the overall motives of Uncle Peck, his Personal Connection throughout the play could be, "When I was pursuing someone I desired but using poor methods."

When playing the scene where Uncle Peck tries to convince Li'l Bit to go to a hotel with him, the actor could have the Essential Action, *to pursue something without regard to acceptable behaviors.* At the time we were rehearsing the play, the actor playing Uncle Peck was able to identify a number of Personal Connections from his own life, including attempting to drink illegally as a teenager or asking someone out on a date, even though he knew she was seeing someone else. A Personal Connection for this actor could be, "When I was pursuing my best friend's girlfriend without regard to acceptable behaviors."

Inexperience vs. Experience

Some have said that an actor cannot achieve excellence until they are at least forty years old and have experienced more of life's challenges. The core reasoning behind this belief is understandable; having an abundance of life experiences to use for empathy and understanding roles can certainly assist the actor. However, it is an extremely limiting belief, denying that there is a craft to acting and negating the use of reliable methods for empathy and imagination. The Essential Action and Personal Connection can be particularly helpful for young actors, whose life experience is significantly less than that of an actor over forty years of age. Many roles that student actors might play require understanding characters with vast and varied life experiences. A young actor in one of my acting classes said:

> *I know it sounds trite, but the biggest sacrifices many of us have made in our lives deal with small material things or time priorities between friends and school work. The biggest risks many of us have taken were in our first serious relationships. We don't yet know what it is like to raise a child or go through a divorce that involves the division of personal belongings or shared time with the kids. Most of us have not felt the anxiety of buying property and dealing with large amounts of debt or of moving an entire family for the sake of a new job. I would venture to guess that many of us have not yet dealt with the loss of close loved ones.*

I believe this student clearly expressed why it is necessary for young actors to use Personal Connections and Essential Actions as a means for empathizing with experiences uncommon to them. For those actors over forty, the experiences of child rearing, divorce, purchasing and possibly dividing property, paying off debt, and asking others to make sacrifices for our professional careers are shared experiences and might even fall into the category of the ordinary. However, any actor will most likely be challenged by roles that require an understanding of such things as murder, being a monarch, disabilities, science fiction, millionaires, fatal diseases, playing non-human characters, death and dying, daring adventures, life-threatening situations, giving birth, and so on. Understanding the use of the Essential Action and Personal Connection methods is absolutely necessary for young actors and certainly an excellent and reliable acting tool for all actors.

Seven Steps for Identifying the Essential Action and Personal Connections

1. Identify the character's objective.

2. Consider which Universal Action is in the objective, using the verb as a guide.

3. Write an Essential Action statement built upon the Universal Action. You need not use the same verb as long as it contains the essence or same general qualities.

4. Identify a Personal Connection by recalling a specific life experience that matches up with the Essential Action.

5. Recall what motivated this life experience and how it felt from beginning to end. Consider all levels of actions and feelings felt at this time.

6. List all actions and emotions you discovered during this recall.

7. Working from this list you created, apply the tactics and Emotional Colors you discovered to your scene score.*

Note: You may find that you need to adjust the intensity levels of some of these tactics and emotions if your life experience was less urgent or not as extreme a situation as the character's experience. Simply select more intense Action Words or Emotional Colors from the same Postural Attitudes or Basic Emotion categories.

[Examples] Essential Actions and Personal Connections for Scene Objectives

To illustrate this process, let's go back to some of the situations and objectives first provided in the Thoughts chapter and see how an actor could apply Essential Action as a method for personally connecting to the experiences of the character. For the sake of brevity, the life situation examples are briefly referred to here and are shorter than you might explore for yourselves.

(1) **Situation:** Agnes in *Agnes of God*. Agnes is a young girl in a nunnery who recently and mysteriously gave birth to a baby. She is being questioned by a psychologist throughout the play about her situation.

Objective:	To verify that God is my baby's father
Universal Action:	To prove
Essential Action:	To prove something beyond the comprehension of another
Personal Connection:	When I tried to prove to my disbelieving friends that I did meet a famous person in my grocery store just down the street

Emotions: Stubborn, proud, irritated, bold, aggravated, baffled, surprised, offended, enthusiastic, optimistic, ecstatic, spirited, festive, brooding, dismayed, and lonely

Action Words: Appeal, claim, entreat, convince, persuade, plead, captivate, recoil, explain, reveal, sustain, and declare

(2) Situation: King Henry in *Henry V.* King Henry is delivering an inspiring speech about how these men will be honored for generations to come for their bravery and valor on this day, Saint Crispin's Day.

Objective: To empower my troops to make history by winning the battle

Universal Action: To encourage

Essential Action: To encourage several to take action in a risky situation

Personal Connection: When I was a camp counselor and needed to empower a group of young campers to paddle down the rapids

Emotions: Sincere, good-hearted, devoted, excited, merry, reveling, spirited, ecstatic, stressed, uncertain, restless, fidgety, passionate, breathless, obsessive, fierce, proud, daring, confident, bold, assured, and adamant

Action Words: Declare, cheer, compliment, reinforce, motivate, stimulate, flatter, excite, brighten, arouse, inspire, lead, nurture, show, persuade, enchant, coax, captivate, and claim

(3) Situation: John Book in *Witness*. John is a NYC detective who is protecting a young Amish boy who witnessed a murder. They are hiding in Amish country with the boy and his family while John heals from a serious gunshot wound.

Objective:	To protect my young witness from the murderers
Universal Action:	To protect
Essential Action:	To protect someone from the actions of those who mean to do harm
Personal Connection:	When my friends and I walked my little brother home from school so the bully would not try to pick a fight with him
Emotions:	Bold, courageous, insistent, malevolent, nonchalant, casual, anxious, restless, nervous, suspicious, disapproving, sly, mischievous, grateful, eager, confident, disappointed, pensive, affectionate, kind, friendly, doting, and compassionate
Action Words:	Confront, assure, advise, search, investigate, lend, comfort, contain, entreat, appeal, soothe, organize, invite, guide, defend, guard, prevent, and harbor

(4) Situation: Robert in *Proof*. Robert is the father of Catherine, a young woman who could be the next mathematical genius but is not motivated to pursue her true talents.

Objective:	To teach her that all things in life are based in numbers
Universal Action:	To share
Essential Action:	To share something in order to enrich someone's life

Personal Connection: When I told my good friend who was struggling with her health about the benefits of a great nutritional program I have used that changed my life

Emotions: Concerned, genial, loving, thankful, enthusiastic, eager, confident, grateful, amazed, obsessive, enticed, fervent, insistent, and assured

Action Words: Convey, disclose, reveal, cheer, encourage, reinforce, incite, urge, coax, convince, captivate, appeal, share, council, and advise

(5) Situation: Shrek in *Shrek.* Shrek is an ogre who wants to regain his isolated living conditions, but he is inundated with unwelcome visitors disrupting his peace.

Objective: To regain control over my home and sanctuary

Universal Action: To reclaim

Essential Action: To reclaim something that was taken from me

Personal Connection: When there was a big party in my apartment and I wanted everyone to leave so I could have my private quiet space back again

Emotions: Sarcastic, stubborn, insistent, fuming, demanding, alarmed, astounded, baffled, offended, flustered, rejoicing, thankful, eager, disappointed, sulking, desolate, fretful, concerned, and amiable

Action Words: Confront, demand, rant, accuse, discharge, ignore, reject, complain, interrogate, intimidate, scorn, threaten, withdraw, declare, maintain, and confess

---

Exercise
Identifying Essential Action and Personal Connections

Now try your hand at identifying the Essential Action and Personal Connection from the scene situations and objectives provided in earlier chapters. Follow the guidelines provided for identifying and wording the Essential Action. Then take the steps that bring you to identifying the Personal Connection and recognizing emotions and actions discovered through this reflection. When you recall the life experience, allow for plenty of detail. Perhaps you could describe the event to someone else or write it as a story or a journal entry. With either method be sure to include plenty of details, particularly with reference to how you behaved and felt.

(1) Situation: Julie in *Miss Julie*. Julie is a wealthy young lady who is attempting to win the affection of the butler, Jean.

Objective: To make him to love me

Universal Action:_____

Essential Action:_____

Personal Connection:_____

_____

Emotions:_____

_____

Action Words:_____

_____

(2) Situation: Claire in *Proof*. Claire is concerned that her sister Catherine is mentally disabled like their father was.

Objective: To protect her from herself

Universal Action:_____

Essential Action:_____

Personal Connection:_____

_____

Emotions:_____

_____

Action Words:_____

_____

(3) Situation: Serge in *Art*. Serge has purchased a very expensive painting and is trying to convince his friends that it was worth the money he spent on it because it is art.

Objective: To prove that this painting is a valued piece of art

Universal Action:_____

Essential Action:_____

Personal Connection:_____

_____

Emotions:_____

_____

Action Words:_____

_____

(4) Situation: Harold Abraham in *Chariots of Fire*. Harold is an Olympic runner who desperately wants to win in the Olympics and honor his Jewish heritage.

Objective: To win the race with honor

Universal Action:_____

Essential Action:_____

Personal Connection:_____

_____

Emotions:_____

_____

Action Words:_____

_____

(5) Situation: Kate in *Taming of the Shrew*. Kate has been married off to Petruchio who is determined to tame the shrew in her. After their long journey to her new home with him, he denies her food as he attempts to get her to speak sweetly to him.

Objective: To do whatever it takes to get him to feed me

Universal Action:_____

Essential Action:_____

Personal Connection:_____

_____

Emotions:_____

_____

Action Words:_____

_____

(6) Situation: Hal in *Proof*. Hal's mentor recently died and left an office filled with paperwork on his recent mathematical research. Hal offers to go through the paperwork to see if there is anything important left behind by his mentor.

Objective: To discover groundbreaking research left by my mentor

Universal Action:_____

Essential Action:_____

Personal Connection:_____

_____

Emotions:_____

_____

Action Words:_____

_____

(7) Situation: Evelyn in _The Shape of Things_. Evelyn is a graduate student in art who has an edgy and daring idea for a thesis project, which requires a naïve human subject.

Objective: To create a provocative and daring thesis project

Universal Action:_____

Essential Action:_____

Personal Connection:_____

_____

Emotions:_____

_____

Action Words:_____

_____

(8) Situation: Meg Jones in _The Big Chill_. Meg is a single woman who wants to be a mother. She asks her friend if she would be willing to let her husband sleep with her once, just so she can have a baby.

Objective: To make a baby with my best friend's willing husband

Universal Action:_____

Essential Action:_____

Personal Connection:_____

_____

Emotions:_____

_____

Action Words:_____

_____

(9) Situation: Blanche in *A Streetcar Named Desire.* Blanche, an overly affected and delicate southern lady, is seeking refuge at her sister's rustic and cramped living quarters in New Orleans. She attempts to win the support and affection of her sister's husband and his friends by showing that she brings class and style to their dismal existence.

Objective: To convince them that I am refreshing company

Universal Action:_____

Essential Action:_____

Personal Connection:_____

_____

Emotions:_____

_____

Action Words:_____

_____

(10) Situation: Nick in *Who's Afraid of Virginia Woolf?* Nick is a new faculty member at a private college. Nick and his wife are visiting the house of a senior faculty member and his wife, who happens to be the eccentric daughter of the college president.

Objective: To secure my new position by befriending a senior faculty member

Universal Action:_____

Essential Action:_____

Personal Connection:_____

Emotions:_____

_____

Action Words:_____

_____

_____

Exercise
Challenging Acting Situations

Take a moment and consider possible situations where you might think, "If I were acting that role I would have a very difficult time understanding how to connect with that character's situation!" Use your imagination, or refer to roles you know in films, stories, or plays. List those situations in the exercise below.

Using the guidelines provided in earlier chapters, identify the core need, objective, Universal Action, and Essential Action for each situation.

Identify a Personal Connection for each situation, and write down a detailed description of what you experienced during this event. Then list the emotions and actions you recognized when recalling this situation from your own personal life.

Situation:_____

Need:_____

Objective:_____

Universal Action: _____

Essential Action: _____

TEAM for Actors

Personal Connection: _____

_____

_____

_____

Emotions: _____

Action Words: _____

Situation: _____

Need: _____

Objective: _____

Universal Action: _____

Essential Action: _____

Personal Connection: _____

_____

_____

_____

Emotions: _____

Action Words: _____

Situation: _____

Need: _____

Objective: _____

Manifestation

Universal Action: _____

Essential Action: _____

Personal Connection: _____

_____

_____

_____

Emotions: _____

Action Words: _____

Situation: _____

Need: _____

Objective: _____

Universal Action: _____

Essential Action: _____

Personal Connection: _____

_____

_____

_____

Emotions: _____

Action Words: _____

The Complete TEAM

With this process of achieving empathy and making Personal Connections, you will build a strong foundation to support full embodiment of a role. All the necessary information about the character's experience has been collected from the script, and you have made clear Personal Connections to the character's situations. The resulting TEAM compilation of information may look like this bridge-to-bridge diagram.

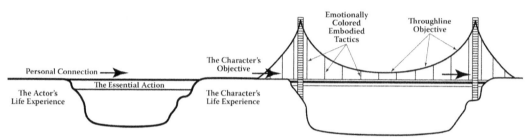

The first simple bridge represents your initial approach to the character's world. The second, more intricate bridge, depicts the multi-layered aspects of analyzing, understanding, and portraying the role. The order in which you explore each section of this process does not necessarily start with the steps indicated on the left side of the bridge diagram and move toward the right side of the diagram. The order of TEAM exploration and development will vary depending on the type of role you are playing, the manner in which you or your director prefers to rehearse, or your own style of approaching acting. Likewise, the techniques you use for embodying these discoveries and revealing actions and reactions in your acting will vary with each occasion, and will often be determined by the preferential approaches of the individual actor.

To help you understand this process, let's apply an Essential Action to the situation of using the TEAM for acting. For purposes of clarity, when TEAM is in all caps, I am referring to TEAM for actors; when not in caps, I am referring to creating a team of people, much like a sports team, or a team of co-workers.

[**Example**] Compare the TEAM with the Essential Action of *forming a strong and diverse team to accomplish a task victoriously.* Building the strong and diverse team is the first step. Creating that team can take time, as potential members are investigated and then join the group as they become available or as they are needed. The most effective teams recognize that all members make valuable and individualized contributions to the success of the ensemble. Each member's skills can be utilized at different times to overcome any challenges that may arise. As the team interacts with other teams, they may need to adjust their methods, try new techniques, and identify different key players, possibly recognizing the strengths of a previously under-utilized member. Then, to accomplish their goal victoriously they would need to raise the stakes, rise to the occasion, and remain unified. This is the essence of TEAM for Actors.

Varying Your Approach and the MVP

Considering the team metaphor we just explored, any given role you play may require a different TEAM MVP (Most Valuable Player). One aspect of the TEAM may be more appropriate for the character's needs. In a case like this, the needs of the character you are playing will dictate the MVP.

[**Example**] You may find that you normally approach your acting roles through emotion, preferring to delve into the feelings and emotional reactions of the character from beat to beat, filling in the rest of the TEAM gradually through rehearsal.

However, another time you may find yourself in a situation where you are playing a character plagued with a serious illness. Throughout the script the character's lines refer to physical symptoms and active behaviors that are directed toward remedying his illness. You may decide that an Action MVP is a more appropriate starting point for your work on this role. You would then research the physical symptoms of the disease, make choices on how the character would respond physically to these symptoms, and take specific actions to resolve the character's serious situation. Later in your rehearsal process, you will discover and fulfill the Emotion and Thought aspects of the TEAM.

With either method, you can use your MVP as an initial rehearsal process, or as a way in to the life of the character. After this initial phase, check that all necessary areas of human behavior have been incorporated and that TEAM is complete so you are producing a fully realized, holistic performance.

TEAM for Actors

Here are some examples of where your use of the TEAM may vary:

• *You have been cast in a production where all players will wear masks. Starting with an Action approach may help you learn to embody the physical characterizations necessary to act through the mask. Then you might connect with the Emotions of the character, which help reveal levels in your modes of expression. Finally, check to see that the Thought motivations of the character are clearly in line with the character's needs and objectives.*

• *You are acting in a film or play that jumps around in time, where you are in the future, then the past, then the present, and back to the future, etc. Starting with a Thought approach may help you anchor each scene in specific needs and objectives, assisting you in tracking the changes in the character in varying times of his life. Then as you gain clarity on this road-mapping technique, you could explore the Actions exhibited by your character during these various phases of his life and finally add how all these elements affect his emotional life.*

• *You have been cast in a role in which the character is disabled in some way. A necessary beginning approach would be following steps in the Manifestation chapter in order to make a Personal Connection with having a disability. Then, researching the disability and how it affects your actions would be an excellent second step in developing this role. Gradually, elements of the character's emotions and needs will arise as you learn how the disability has affected all aspects of her life.*

• *You are acting a role from a script that uses very intricate language. A Thought approach could be applied to investigate subtle and illusive references throughout the script. Approaching scripts written in verse or those that elude to the character's situation using subtle references and lyrical dialogue will take a great deal of advance analysis before you can even consider Actions and Emotions.*

• *You are playing a role where your character is in an abusive situation. You may want to approach this first by scoring the moments with emotions, both as Emotional Colors in reaction to the situation and as Emotion Tactics used as a survival technique for the character. Then consider any physical effects the abuse may have on your character, as well as Action Tactics taken to deal with the situation. Eventually, you will want to check that your choices are in line with all evidence supporting objectives and victories.*

Try This:

Create a list of challenging roles from various plays and films that you know well. Consider which TEAM MVP might best serve your approach to each role. Why would this initial element of the TEAM better serve that role, play, or film? What element of the TEAM might be a good choice for your second level of investigation, and why?

Side Coaching the TEAM

Using a side coach is an excellent process for bringing a score to life, or embodying your TEAM elements, in rehearsal. I use side coaches all the time in my acting classes and at some point in the rehearsal process of a play. The side coach is someone who stands closely on the side lines of your rehearsal space with your score in hand. This person acts as your personal coach, watching your performance while referring to your scene score. Your coach calls out choices you have made in writing to remind you, in the moment of your acting, to embody them.

This is similar to the immediate feedback given by a basketball coach standing on the sidelines of a practice session, calling out reminders to team members. The TEAM side coach serves a similar purpose in a rehearsal. However, the TEAM coach works with one actor and reinforces only one aspect of the TEAM at a time, like Emotion Tactics, so you do not become overwhelmed with too many layers to focus on at once. If the coach does not see you embody these choices, he will continue to call out the Emotion Tactic until he sees evidence of it in your performance. Your coach can also remind you of your Scene Objective by calling it out whenever he believes you have lost sight of your desired victory. This coaching process helps you recognize if your choices are manifesting clearly in the performance and not getting stuck "in your head."

Side Coaches for the Tennessee Williams' Play Festival

While directing a Tennessee Williams' one-act play festival, I decided to use side coaches in the rehearsal process for six short plays. The festival provided the perfect opportunity for the student actors to experience what it is like to utilize side coaches as a technique for bringing their scene scores into immediate action. Each short play had small casts of two or three characters, and side coaches could be actors from one of the other short plays.

In the play Hello from Bertha, *the protagonist, Bertha, is an aging and deathly ill prostitute who will not leave her room at the brothel, much to her fellow housemates' frustration. Two other prostitutes keep entering Bertha's room and try to convince her to leave, so they can make her room more profitable to the brothel.*

The actor playing Bertha made the decision that her character was dying of syphilis. After researching the symptoms of the disease and first applying a physical approach to the role, incorporating the specific pains and behaviors of people in states of delirium, she was ready to add the layer of Emotion Tactics. The actor realized that since her character was confined to a bed through the majority of the play, most of the tactics would be emotional. She also realized that the play was written with extremely quick shifts in emotional tone, climaxing to a point in the play where the character escapes into her delirious nostalgic memories of her long lost beau, Charlie.

In order to embody these Emotional Colors and Tactics, she scored her script using the basic emotions. She supported this choice by stating that a character in such an extreme stage of decline and desperation would probably express much of her emotional life in high levels of primary emotional states.

The side coaching of the basic emotions worked perfectly for this role. Her coach crouched down near the bed she was lying in and quietly yet insistently called out each emotion quickly as she shifted from one extreme to the next. As the actor approached the climax of the scene, her coach not only called out the basic emotions in her beats but also coached her to go to higher levels of each emotion in order to reach and punctuate the arc of the play.

It only took a couple rehearsals with the side coaching process for this actor to retain dynamic shifts throughout this exhausting play. Eventually her side coach simply watched and took notes, and the two would confer after each run-through to discuss any places she was forgetting to apply specific choices. The actor also made additional changes in her score between rehearsals as she reflected on areas that needed further development. She would then ask her coach at the next rehearsal to call out only these new choices in the run-through so she would remember the change and test its effectiveness in the moment.

This process was mesmerizing to witness, and the final performance this actor produced had audiences riveted all the way to the end of this tour-de-force role!

Try This:

Take a scene from any play or movie script that interests you, and complete a score sheet with an objective and beats marked with Subtext Statements and Emotion and Action Tactics. Perform the scene with a scene partner and add side coaches to remind you of your choices, one element at a time. Then change some of your tactics or Subtext Statements and perform the scene all over again with side coaches reminding you of the new choices. Discuss with your coach which choices seemed to work the best and why. This is good practice to do on a regular basis. Eventually, this process may become habitual, and you may find you start to automatically apply and test variations of dynamic choices in your acting process.

Guidelines for Using a Side Coach

1. Make sure your score is easy to read. Clearly indicate the beginning and end of each beat by drawing a horizontal line across the script between each beat.

2. Mark beat titles (Subtext Statement, Emotion Tactic, Postural Attitude, or Action Tactic) in specific columns. Color code, or use small colored sticky notes for the different aspects of the TEAM.

3. Side coaching works best at a point in the rehearsal where you are truly "off-book," or have your lines well memorized. Receiving side coaching requires that your attention is on the interactions in the scene and on receiving information from your coach. If you are thinking too much about what your next line is, you will find you are unable to rehearse with a side coach effectively.

4. Ask your side coach to call out only one beat title category (for example, the Subtext Statements) for a given rehearsal or run-through.

5. If the coach repeats the same beat title, try to embody that choice more, or explore another way to express the choice so your coach can recognize it in your acting and interacting.

6. If you can't hear your coach, say, "Louder, Coach!" while remaining in character, and repeat where necessary.

7. Feel free to take a beat over again if you hear that your coach is not seeing your choices manifested in your performance. There is no need to continue to the end of the scene if you are not embodying your score from beat to beat. If you find that your coach is repeating a beat title more than once, you may want to stop, back up, and take a beat over again, trying a different way to embody your choice.

8. Even if you knew your lines well before side coaching, you might lose some of your lines here and there as you concentrate on the

coaching and the interactions with others in the scene. If this happens, simply call to your coach, "Line!" while staying in character. Your coach will then call out your lines until you are able to pick the scene back up again.

9. If a beat title you chose previously is now feeling like an odd choice for the moment, stop and ask your coach to write down a note that you want to change that beat title. You can either change it in the moment, or later when you talk over your work with your coach.

10. Remember that your side coach is there to support you, to reflect and reinforce the intellectual choices you made in preparation. Receiving side coaching is an intense exercise that takes patience, concentration, and a willingness to receive information outside of your acting space. Remain open and receptive to the process. The payoff in the end is tremendous.

Guidelines for Serving as a Side Coach

1. Look over the score sheet of the actor you are coaching, and make sure you are clear on which beat titles you are calling out and where beats begin and end. Ask for clarification if you can't read someone's handwriting or if a beat or title is not clear to you.

2. Stay close to the edge of the acting area, on the side of the stage closest to your actor. If the actor moves to another part of the stage, try to move to that side of the stage as well. Do not step into their acting space.

3. Call out only what is written on the actor's score sheet. Do not add anything or comment on their acting. Your job is to simply reinforce what the actor wrote on the score sheet and what the actor has asked you to call out.

4. When calling out beat titles, try to call them quickly and with clear articulation. Deliver the coaching in between lines, when possible.

5. Use a volume that is loud enough for the actor to hear. Sometimes coaches may be shy about talking too loudly, worried they are interfering with the acting. Talking too softly can actually be more distracting and disruptive, causing the actor to literally lean away from their acting work, trying to figure out what the coach said. Remember, the actor asked you to be a coach. You have been given permission to call these titles out.

6. If an actor calls to you, "Louder, Coach!" give your coaching at a louder volume. Try to match the volume and the emotional intensity of the actors in the scene.

7. If you do not see evidence of the actor applying the choice you called out, repeat it. The actor may not have heard you or may not be embodying that choice clearly enough for audience members to see. If you see the evidence but sense it is too subtle, continue to call the beat title until it is produced with greater intensity, particularly in identified arcs or climaxes of the scene.

8. If an actor calls to you, "Line!" call out their line as quickly as you can. Deliver a full sentence of their lines and then wait to see them pick up from there. If they don't, continue with the next sentence. If they start talking over you, then simply stop the delivery. Never feed an actor a line unless they ask you to with the "Line!" command. This is standard and accepted practice in theatre line coaching.

9. After the scene is over, meet with your actor and go over any areas of the score that seem to be less evident in the acting. Help the actor identify ongoing patterns. For example, if whenever the actor is expressing anger she is mixing in fear as well, tell her of this observation. You may also help her recognize repetitious beat titles where other options may help make the scene become more diversified and dynamic.

10. If you want to offer advice or suggestions, always ask first by saying something like, "I have an opinion about a beat title, would you like

to hear it?" Or "Are you open to suggestions for beat titles to help make the arc more dynamic?" When giving your own advice or suggestions, make sure you are talking specifically about beat titles and objectives. Resist the temptation to tell or show the actor how to act the moment. Remember, you are a side coach who is there to support the preparatory choices the actor has made in advance. You are helping the actor test and adjust the effectiveness of these choices in performance. You are not the director of this scene.

Recommended Progression with Side Coaches

Step One: Run the scene with a side coach calling out objective reminders or the beat titles for one element of the TEAM (Beat Subtext, Emotion Tactic, Postural Attitude, or Action Tactic).

Step Two: After the first run-through with a coach, make any adjustments needed on the score and run the scene again with side coaching. With this step, either the coach can call out every beat title for this element of the TEAM, or the actor can ask the coach to only call out beat titles that the coach is not seeing exhibited in the acting.

Step Three: After reviewing any changes in the score, and once the scene gets to a point where very little side coaching is needed, the coach can simply watch and take notes on any beats that still need more clarity.

To work on a new element of the TEAM, go back to Step One, calling out the new element and follow through to Step Three.

Director's Use of Side Coaching

When a director is using side coaches as part of the rehearsal process, the director needs to allow for side coach and actor conferencing after each scene is completed. It is also best to delay any actor directing during this process. It could be very overwhelming for an actor to receive commentary from a coach <u>and</u> from a director during a side coaching rehearsal. The director may find that the coaching process will resolve many acting issues observed previously, and because of this, actors may end up needing very few directorial notes after a rehearsal with coaches. During a coaching rehearsal, it is best for the director to simply orchestrate the coaching process and reserve notes for another rehearsal when coaches are not in Steps One and Two of the coaching process.

The TEAM in Practice

While developing the TEAM in my Acting II Scene Study class over the years, I was always thrilled to see how the technique encouraged independence and proactivity in the student actors. In the days before I developed the technique, actors seemed lost and confused about making the most basic acting choices, and they waited to be told how to work the scene.

Now my acting classes buzz with activity as students work in groups all over our large acting studio. After a couple weeks of instruction on how to apply the TEAM theories, individual actors arrive for class with a scene score prepared and lines memorized to work on their first short scene. Then scene partners work together, comparing beat titles, clarifying objectives, and identifying the arc of the scene. They practice their beat title choices, explore embodiment techniques, and then hover over their scene scores again, making revisions. Finally groups of four students form together as another pair of actors serve as side coaches for a scene. The room swells with excitement as the groups apply side coaching, and the studio erupts into insistent calls out to actors, pushing them to make committed choices. Laughter, encouraging cheers, and expressions of gratitude for coaching support echo throughout the class. I wander from scene to scene, observing their work growing stronger with each run-through.

The classroom techniques we practice in Acting II eventually move to theatre rehearsals as we work to produce a play for our main stage. We are producing short Tennessee Williams' plays. One of the plays, The Lady of Larkspur Lotion, *has a cast of three playing the characters of the Lady of Larkspur, the Writer, and the Landlady. Within this cast, two actors have had the Acting II class, and one—the actor playing the Landlady—has not. All the actors have been sent instructions on how to prepare their scores and have been informed when they should be off-book to work with coaches. As the coaches—from another cast of Williams' plays—arrive for the first night of side coaching, I witness nervous looks from the actor playing the Landlady. She has never worked in this manner before and appears to be anxious and unsure of its benefits. I decide to partner an experienced coach with her.*

Those who are familiar with this process eagerly welcome their assigned coaches and start going over their scores. We prepare to run a scene with Step One of the side coaching process. Three coaches line the edges of the stage, one crouching low in a corner, another sitting toward the front of the closest seat near her actor, ready to launch into action when needed. The third stands with legs spread wide, leaning toward the stage action, ready to start his calls. All three coaches hold their actors' individual scores and wait, anxiously, like runners at the starting block.

The scene starts and a flurry of quick coaching calls fly out to the actors as they begin the first beat. The coaching calls become staggered as the scene progresses and coaches work with the varying lengths of their actors' beats. Occasionally we hear an actor call out "Louder, Coach!" or "Line!" One actor experienced in this process breaks for a brief moment and asks for an Emotion Tactic title change:

"Coach, can you change that choice from surprised to exhilarated?"

"Sure thing!" says the coach as a quick note is jotted down.

"Thank you!" expresses the actor, and the scene resumes.

As we reach the arc of the scene, the coach partnered with the Landlady paces back and forth, following his actor who has a lot of movement in the scene. The coach looks much like the border collie, nipping at the heels of a sheep as he realizes he needs to continuously call out the same beat title. The Landlady looks like she is not doing much more than pacing and spitting out lines.

"Intimidate," the coach calls to the actor.

"Intimidate!" he calls again, not seeing much intimidation.

The actor playing the Landlady just chooses to get louder with her line, thinking that is enough to intimidate.

"In-tim-i-date!!" the coach pushes.

Finally the actor exhibits a strong move, using a fully embodied combination of voice, gesture, proximity, and emotion that is completely committed and indeed intimidating to the character of the Writer. The Landlady holds her ground, towering over the Writer. The moment is captivating. The Writer is now raising his stakes, feeling the fear, wanting to flee, but his coach calls a Postural Attitude and Action Tactic, "1A and Guard." The third actor, playing the Lady of Larkspur, is standing on the edge of the acting space and is coached with a Shift Subtext, "I knew he wouldn't be able to protect me!" and she looks on in dismay and disgust. The resulting moment is a riveting stand-off, with the Lady of Larkspur adding an extra layer of reaction to the scene. The actors hold this moment for a beat, and the stage manager calls, "And...scene!" as this scene unit ends.

Coaches rush up to their actors and congratulate them on work well done, and they begin to pore over scores with notes. The Landlady grabs her coach and gives him a big bear hug: "Thank you! Thank you for pushing me! I've never been able to get that moment as strong as it was this time! I love my coach!" She hugs him again, and then they sit to review her score.

Later in the week that same actor playing the Landlady will have the opportunity to coach another actor in a different play, and she will learn what it is like to be on the other side of the TEAM coaching process and, in fact, learn more about her own acting while she does so.

As the rehearsals progress, the designated side coaching nights are eagerly welcomed by actors. As coaches arrive, productive exchanges of ideas are abundant throughout the theatre. I find that whenever it is a Step One or Step Two side coaching night I can just sit and enjoy watching the process, witnessing incredible acting growth occurring with everyone on stage, all at once. It is gratifying, and I realize this process makes our acting ensemble a stronger and tighter team than I have ever witnessed before.

Bubbling Up after Side Coaching

Side coaching the TEAM is intended as a training and rehearsing technique for developing an actor's skill in actively applying scene scores and incorporating the whole self in acting. Let's compare this to a martial arts class where repetitive movements, designed to prepare a person for moments of physical conflict, are drilled over and over again. The martial arts pupil learns both active and reactive movements as well as counter strategies designed to steer the confrontation in a desired direction. Through repetitive application and by connecting basic movements to strategic tactical theories, the individual can rely on this training to become ingrained and to essentially rise up impulsively when needed.

Now relate this martial arts process, and its intended results, to using side coaches for applying the TEAM to acting. The goal with side coaching is to provide a support system for the actor to integrate intellectual script analysis choices and theories into embodied action. The side coaching technique provides a process for moving from page to stage and for merging thoughts, emotions, and actions. Ultimately, the actor must eventually trust the preparatory work, let go of the conscious application, and allow these choices to emerge as subconscious impulses and interactions.

I often refer to this result as Bubbling Up, like a pot of water going from simmer to pre-boil to boil. The surface of the water may appear still while simmering. However, underneath that surface, tiny beads of activity and small waves of movement start pulsing from the bottom and rise to the top. If we watch people in common interpersonal exchanges, they display various levels of behavior that reveal their needs. We can see the truth of these needs subtly simmering in their postures, gestures, and moods. Larger reactions to given circumstances can rise like a quick boil, breaking through the social mask layer, revealing unguarded reactions.

As you merge the theories and techniques of the TEAM into your acting, keep in mind that the objective of this book is to become one of your favorite acting companions. These methods want to be used regularly in acting rehearsals, in classes, and during personal reading and preparation time. However, you must eventually trust the process, immerse yourself in the given circumstances of the role, and individuate from the book, side coaches, and director so that it is possible to fully embody the part.

Embodying the TEAM

Many actors train in various techniques for years, hoping to diversify their embodiment methods as well as find one or two approaches that work best with their own personal acting preferences. Knowing that many diverse techniques exist, actor training programs will either (1) dedicate their curriculum to a detailed exploration of one approach or (2) provide multiple experiential courses or workshops introducing a variety of embodiment options. This second approach often refers to these options as "tools for the actor's toolbox."

You may already have favorite methods for embodiment, or you may find that embodying comes easily by simply imagining yourself in the character's situations and "playing those moments." In these cases you may be able to fully embody the TEAM immediately. The side coaching techniques are designed to reinforce and provide feedback on the actor's expression and physicalization of the TEAM. However, if you find that further study of embodiment methods are needed, or if you would like to learn additional techniques for manifesting the choices introduced in this text, an alphabetical list of some embodiment techniques (with their originator listed in parentheses) follows. These techniques can be explored for further study and investigation of embodying the TEAM or used as companions to the TEAM.

When learning any somatic or embodiment technique, it is best to have an experienced instructor working with you to help you see and understand the intricacies of the technique's application and provide you with feedback on your progress. I encourage you to look up these techniques and work with an experienced or certified instructor specializing in these methods.

- Alba Emoting *(Susana Bloch)*
- Grotowski on Physical Actions *(Jerzy Growtowski)*
- Meisner Technique *(Sanford Meisner)*
- Michael Chekhov Technique *(Michael Chekhov)*
- Spolin Technique *(Viola Spolin)*
- Stanislavski System *(Constantine Stanislavski)*
- Suzuki Method of Actor Training *(Tadashi Suzuki)*
- Uta Hagen's Teachings *(Uta Hagen)*
- Viewpoints Method *(Anne Bogart & Tina Landau)*

Conclusion

TEAM for Actors reveals valuable insights into your acting process, and provides step-by-step methods that you can use for years to come in your work as an actor, creating roles that are holistically embodied. Specific techniques used in this book will assist you in identifying the multi-layered aspects of behavior in the characters you play and will reinforce the importance of employing all elements of the TEAM in your acting.

By studying and practicing the lessons on basic human behavior, motivation theories, and steps for empathizing with another person's story, you will gain invaluable skills that can serve you both on and off stage. The concepts in this book can help you make infinite discoveries about yourself, your acting, and the interactions of people around you.

Take your time to absorb the ideas and techniques provided here. Practice the Exercises and "Try This" explorations at home alone, or in cooperation with others through partner work, in rehearsals for a performance, or in classroom scene studies. Find a trusted individual to work with you as your own personal TEAM side coach, or use this book as your coach by making notes in the margins and actively using the checklists and score sheets to prepare a role. When rereading the stories of how the TEAM was developed and used, try imagining yourself in those situations, or keep a journal about your own personal discoveries and your use of the TEAM.

Remember, *TEAM for Actors* is a process used to achieve a fully embodied and believable performance, where the technique used for its creation eventually becomes invisible to the audience and simply looks dynamic and true. The actor's instrument is complex and multi-layered and yet can be tuned as finely as a violin to play exquisite scenes.

Play on!

Appendix A
Checklists

Victory Statement Checklist

☐ Is the victory placed in the actions of your scene partner?

☐ Is the victory stated in the second person: "He will…" or "She will…"?

☐ Is the victory stated in positive terms of what will be done, not what won't be done?

☐ Is the statement kept to one simple sentence with one action verb and one subject?

☐ Is the victory in line with the intentions of the Scene Objective?

☐ Is the victory challenging to achieve, but conceivable?

☐ If the victory is accomplished, is it achieved by the very end of the scene?

Main Objective Checklist

☐ Is it anchored in a basic human need?

☐ Does it focus on one single outcome?

☐ Does it utilize only one Action Word?

☐ Does it motivate your actions throughout the play/movie?

☐ Is it supported by the events in your character's scenes?

☐ Is it stated in positive terms, focusing on what you want, not what you don't want?

☐ Is it a short, single-subject phrase, stated in the first person?

☐ Is the achievement of the outcome difficult, taking the entire action of the play/movie to accomplish, if accomplished at all?

☐ Is there a specific victory that would end all actions toward this outcome?

Scene Objective Checklist

☐ Is it anchored in a basic human need?

☐ Does it focus on one single outcome?

☐ Does it utilize only one Action Word?

☐ Does it motivate your actions throughout the entire scene?

☐ Does it contribute to your character's Main Objective?

☐ Does it include the need for your scene partner's participation?

☐ Is it stated in positive terms, focusing on what you want, not what you don't want?

☐ Is it a short, single-subject phrase, stated in the first person?

☐ Does the desire for the outcome have great immediate urgency?

☐ Is the achievement of the outcome challenging but conceivable?

☐ Is there a specific victory that would end all actions toward this outcome?

Super Objective Checklist

☐ Is it anchored in a basic human need?

☐ Does it focus on one single outcome?

☐ Does it utilize only one Action Word?

☐ Does it motivate your actions throughout and well beyond the action of the script?

☐ Is it supported by your character's Main Objective?

☐ Is it stated in positive terms, focusing on what you want, not what you don't want?

☐ Is it a short, single-subject phrase, stated in the first person?

☐ Is the achievement of the outcome extremely difficult, taking nearly a lifetime to accomplish?

☐ Is there a specific victory that would end all actions toward this outcome?

Door Visualization Checklist

☐ How I will appear to those witnessing my actions

☐ What they will think of me

☐ What I will do

☐ What they will do in return

☐ What I will say

☐ What they will say in return

☐ What I will get in the end

Subtext Statement Checklist

☐ Is the subtext written in a short phrase or sentence?

☐ Is the subtext encased in quotes to clarify it is from your character's perspective?

☐ Does the content of the subtext capture the essence of the changing subject, Emotion Tactic, or Action Tactic?

☐ Does the tone of the subtext express strong, honest feelings about the situation?

☐ Is the thought or feeling expressed in the subtext in line with the goals of your character's objective?

Guidelines for Choosing Emotion Tactics

☐ Select a singular word that reflects a feeling, emotion, or state of being.

☐ Select words that appear to stem from basic emotions.

☐ Fully understand the meaning of the word used and how it would affect your character's state of emotional being.

☐ Steer clear of words that are too intellectual, keeping you from full embodiment.

☐ Keep in mind basic emotions that reflect your character's core personality traits, preferred social mask, and darker shadow self.

☐ Use the Subtext Statement to guide your Emotion Tactic choices.

☐ Allow as many Emotional Colors and Emotion Tactics in a beat as necessary for actions, reactions, and impulses to occur.

☐ Consider the arc of the scene when selecting Emotion Tactics throughout the scene.

☐ Consider opposites, or antithetical thinking, when selecting emotion words so you don't select obvious or trite choices.

Checklist for Choosing Action Tactics

☐ Use specific Action Words to title your tactics; avoid generalized verbs.

☐ Make sure each new beat has a distinctly new Action Tactic.

☐ Build your Action Word vocabulary to encompass a wide range of actions, and fully understand the meaning of the word used.

☐ Steer clear of words that are highly intellectual, simply emotional, or existential.

☐ Use your Action Words to reflect your character's conscious choices of action toward the Scene Objective.

Seven Steps for identifying the Essential Action and Personal Connections

1. Identify the character's objective.

2. Consider which Universal Action is in the objective, using the verb as a guide.

3. Write an Essential Action statement built upon the Universal Action. You need not use the same verb as long as it contains the essence or same general qualities.

4. Identify a Personal Connection by recalling specific life experiences that match up with the Essential Action.

5. Recall what motivated this life experience and how it felt from beginning to end. Consider all levels of actions and feelings felt at this time.

6. List all actions and emotions you discovered during this recall.

7. Working from this list you created, apply the tactics and Emotional Colors you discovered to your scene score.*

*Note: You may find that you need to adjust the intensity levels of some of these tactics and emotions if your life experience was less urgent or not as extreme a situation as the character's experience. Simply select more intense Action Words or Emotional Colors from the same Postural Attitudes or Basic Emotion categories.

OPEN SCENE

Use this scene to exercise your use of Objectives, Needs, Victories, Emotion and Action Tactics, Subtext, and Postural Attitudes.

A: Hi.

B: Hello.

A: Great outfit.

B: Thanks.

A: Where did you get it?

B: It's my own.

A: Your own?

B: Yes. Mine.

A: Wow!

B: Thanks.

A: I mean it.

B: Well – again, thanks.

A: So? I was wondering…

B: Wondering?

A: If you could…

B: Really?

A: Do you mind?

B: No.

A: No? …. Or No?

B: No.

A: All right then.

B: Ok.

Appendix C
Scenes for Practice

Scene from *Vassal...Vegetable* by Sam Post

This is a sample scene for the Emotions Chapter or can be used for general scene study practice by creating your own beat scores.

You can disregard the Trish/Bill gender references to allow for more flexibility in scene study work.

The following scene is from the ten-minute play *Vassal...Vegetable* by Sam Post (printed in this text with permission from Sam Post) For the rest of this play, or to read more plays by Sam Post go to www.sampost.com or purchase his book, *An Actor's Dozen: Thirteen Quick and Easy Ten Minute Plays.*

Character's Basic Need:_____

Character's Scene Objective: _____

Victory Statement: _____

Possible beat scores to exercise: Shift Subtext Statements, Emotion Tactics, Emotional Colors, Action Tactics, and Postural Attitudes.

Beat Scores

Beat #	Script Text			
	TRISH packs books into boxes. BILL watches. She lifts a book and stops. **TRISH** This. **BILL** Huh?			

Beat #	Script Text			
	TRISH This dictionary. **BILL** What about it? **TRISH** It's not mine. **BILL** Yes it is. **TRISH** Bill, it's not. **BILL** Whose is it? **TRISH** I don't know, but this one isn't mine. **BILL** It's a dictionary. It's yours. **TRISH** I want to know what happened to mine. **BILL** Nothing. That's it. **TRISH** Mine was older, and there was masking tape on it. **BILL** That's your dictionary.			

Beat Scores

Beat #	Script Text			
	TRISH I had words underlined. **BILL** Why? **TRISH** It doesn't matter why. I did it. They're there. **BILL** Silly. They're in alphabetical order. **TRISH** They're my words. Words I looked up, in my dictionary. **BILL** Well... **TRISH** I want them back. **BILL** There it is. **TRISH** I've had my dictionary at least five years. The cover fell off. I taped it with masking tape. This one doesn't have tape. **BILL** It's the same thing. **TRISH** It's not the same edition.			

Beat Scores

Beat #	Script Text			
	BILL It looks the same to me. It's a Webster's Paperback. **TRISH** This isn't my copy. **BILL** The words are the same. **TRISH** How do you know? **BILL** I read parts of it. **TRISH** My words were marked. **BILL** This is the same. **TRISH** I don't think it is. **BILL** It is. I know. **TRISH** Admit it. This isn't my copy. You know it isn't. **BILL** Okay, I admit it's a different copy. But it's the same book. Same cover, page numbers, everything. **TRISH** What happened to mine?			

Beat #	Script Text			
	BILL I borrowed it, and I lost it. **TRISH** No you didn't. **BILL** You don't believe me. **TRISH** No! **BILL** The important thing is that you've got a dictionary. **TRISH** I need to know what you did with mine. **BILL** Suppose that's something you'll never know. **TRISH** You don't use dictionaries. **BILL** Apparently I do. **TRISH** You knew it was important. That's why you did something to it. **BILL** And...I got you that one. I cared about it.			

Beat Scores

Beat #	Script Text			
	TRISH That one's not the important one. Mine is important. **BILL** There's no difference. **TRISH** I looked up a lot of words in my dictionary. That was my…I took pride in…it was getting worn out. I was using it up, you fucker. What happened to my dictionary! *pause* **BILL** What's the time frame on this departure? **TRISH** A day. **BILL** How about if I just come back tomorrow? **TRISH** You need to stay here to answer questions about my stuff. **BILL** All your stuff is here. **TRISH** You might have stolen other stuff.			

Beat Scores

Beat #	Script Text			
	BILL I didn't steal anything. **TRISH** I want you around for the rest of the surprises. In case there's other stuff gone. **BILL** Have I ever stolen anything? **TRISH** Just now. **BILL** There aren't any surprises. **TRISH** I don't know that. **BILL** And what if there are? **TRISH** If there are, you need to be here. **BILL** If there are surprises, they will... you know...as soon as you find out about them...they won't be surprises anymore. **TRISH** That's a mirror for your life, right there. You throw these things out, but they don't matter to you— because to you—they aren't surprises.			

Beat #	Script Text			
	BILL A mirror for my life. Stuff like that...making so much of things like this, the dictionary...mirrors —that's a mirror for yours. *pause* **TRISH** Mine? **BILL** Yeah. **TRISH** Making...more of things. **BILL** Yeah. **TRISH** Imagining things? **BILL** Yeah. **TRISH** Like the dictionary. **BILL** Uh huh. **TRISH** I'm just now learning how far you're willing to go. **BILL** See? It's what you do. Little things get way, way off. Like you throw			

Beat #	Script Text			
	buckets of paint on things—make them your own color. This will be good for me. **TRISH** I don't think so. **BILL** You don't. **TRISH** I've got a hole in my heart…it's like…this big…She displays the dictionary—or bigger. You put it there. I'll go ahead and break the news to you right now, Bill: when you do it to the next person… make another hole like this…it won't be good for her either, or you…anybody. **BILL** Imagination—just like I said. **TRISH** I could show you something that you would not like to see. And it would have nothing to do with imagination. **BILL** You could. **TRISH** Sure could, and will. **BILL** You'll show me something.			

Beat Scores

Beat #	Script Text			
	TRISH Yourself. *sarcastic* **BILL** Frightening. **TRISH** I know you don't care. **BILL** I don't know what you're talking about. **TRISH** You know, but you think it's a simple thing: I say something mean, to hurt you…and it doesn't hurt. You know it. Right? **BILL** Yeah. **TRISH** Because you can hurt me, and it doesn't go in the other direction. **BILL** Whatever you say, Trish.			

Scene from *Poochie* by Sam Post

This is a sample scene for the Emotions Chapter or can be used for general scene study practice by creating your own beat scores.

You can disregard the Nate/Jim gender references to allow for more flexibility in scene study work.

The following scene is from the full length play *Poochie* by Sam Post (printed in this text with permission from Sam Post) To read more plays by Sam Post go to www.sampost.com or purchase his book, *An Actor's Dozen: Thirteen Quick and Easy Ten Minute Plays.*

Character's Basic Need:_____

Character's Scene Objective: _____

Victory Statement: _____

Possible beat scores to exercise: Shift Subtext Statements, Emotion Tactics, Emotional Colors, Action Tactics, and Postural Attitudes.

Beat Scores

Beat #	Script Text			
	(Late at night. JIM enters and turns on the light. He's wearing pajamas, carrying a sandwich. He picks up the remote, surfs channels for a few seconds, and takes a bite.) (Moments later, **NATE** enters. He's wearing boxer shorts.)			

Beat Scores

Beat #	Script Text			
	NATE Caught 'cha. **JIM** *(chewing, he looks up)* A little hungry. **NATE** Good sandwich? **JIM** Tuna salad. Too much celery in it. **NATE** Celery's good. Gives it the crunch. **JIM** Too much annoys me. **NATE** A celery sandwich with a little tuna in it. **JIM** That's it. **NATE** Wouldn't bother me. **JIM** It might. **NATE** I don't eat tuna salad much, so I don't have some ideal that I compare it to. Whatever way it shows up is perfect to me. You know. That's me. Whereas you've			

Beat #	Script Text			
	got this vision of perfection—the correct amount of tuna and mayo and celery. You'll never be satisfied, you know? For you, it's not even a sandwich, really. **JIM** It's not a sandwich. **NATE** No it's not. **JIM** Excuse me? **NATE** It's not a sandwich. **JIM** Then what is it? **NATE** It's just, you know, another disappointment that you're calling a sandwich. **JIM** This is a disappointment. **NATE** Yeah. **JIM** And not a sandwich. **NATE** If it were, you'd eat it.			

Beat Scores

Beat #	Script Text			
	JIM I am eating it. **NATE** What you're eating there is a concept. **JIM** I'm eating a concept. **NATE** Yeah—after you talk about it, and describe it, and evaluate it—you don't really have a sandwich anymore. You don't get to really enjoy it. *(He takes a bite.)* **JIM** It's okay. **NATE** Yeah—it's okay. But it's not a sandwich. **JIM** It's bread with tuna, celery, and mayonnaise. I call that a sandwich. **NATE** It was a sandwich. Now it's a list of ingredients.			

Beat Scores

Beat #	Script Text			
	JIM It was ingredients. Now, it's a sandwich! I call it a sandwich. **NATE** It's not in the realm of sandwiches. It's like government. Our constitution is a government for the people, by the people—you know—but people talk about Obama like he's the president. **JIM** Obama is the president. **NATE** Not the way people talk about him. People turn Obama into a list of ingredients too. Same thing with churches. **JIM** Then what the hell is this? **NATE** What? **JIM** Are we talking about a sandwich? **NATE** No! That's what I'm trying to tell you. You take a perfectly good sandwich—tuna salad, right?—and put it into a different realm. You			

Beat #	Script Text			
	take all the sandwich out of the sandwich. **JIM** *(offering the sandwich)* Here—you want it? **NATE** No thanks. **JIM** Take it. **NATE** I'm not asking for your sandwich. **JIM** Seriously—if you're hungry, you can have it. **NATE** I'm not hungry. **JIM** Then leave me alone. It helps me sleep. **NATE** That doesn't help you sleep. **JIM** Yes. It does. **NATE** That's backwards. It's something to eat while you're awake.			

Beat Scores

Beat #	Script Text			
	JIM Does it occur to you what's going on here? **NATE** Nothing's going on. **JIM** Something is going on. You're the one who's not sleeping. **NATE** I stay up. I'm a musician and a poet. **JIM** Well, what are you talking to me for? I'm not your next song. **NATE** You never know.			

Appendix D

Possible Answers to Exercises

Thoughts Chapter, Exercise on pages 45-49

Possible answers for the Basic Needs Motivating Objectives Exercise:
(1) Social (2) Security (3) Beauty (4) Spiritual (5) Ego (6) Body (7) Security (8) Ego (9) Cognitive (10) Ego (11) Fulfillment (12) Body (13) Social (14) Security (15) Social

Thoughts Chapter, Exercise on pages 60-62

Answers to: This Objective Statement is a weak choice because...

(3) This statement uses a passive action of "to be" and is not based in a strong human need.

(4) This statement refers to what the character does not want, putting too much emphasis on the negative.

(5) This statement uses "want" and "to be," both inactive words denying external actions. The statement also includes two desires "to be rich" and "for him to marry me," causing a divided focus.

(6) This statement indirectly refers to something the character does not want and is more of a tactic than an objective.

(7) This statement is active and includes the necessary actions of another; however, there are two desired outcomes. Signing the autograph is a tactic used toward the ultimate desired outcome of getting a date.

(8) This statement does not include the necessary actions of anyone else and has no sense of urgency.

(9) This statement leaves too many questions. From whom or what must the character be protected?

(10) This statement uses "want" as an inactive word choice as well as not requiring the reactions of another to provide a desired result.

Possible Rewording of Weak Objective Statements

(3) To be left alone—<u>To persuade the group to honor my need to concentrate right now</u>

(4) I don't want him ask me out. —<u>To get him to agree that we are better off as friends</u>

(5) I want to be rich and for him to marry me. —<u>To achieve an enviable life style</u>

(6) To avoid being made fun of—<u>To gain their respect for my nonconformist ways</u>

(7) To get her to sign her autograph on my program and agree to go out with me—<u>To get her to agree to go out with me tonight</u>

(8) To eat—<u>To coerce her into giving me her lunch bag before the bus stops</u>

(9) To protect myself—<u>To free myself from his attack</u>

(10) I want to be beautiful.—<u>To gain their acknowledgement of my beauty</u>

Thoughts Chapter, Exercise on pages 70-74

Possible Answers for Building an Objective Statement

(1) Social Need, To gain —To gain her acceptance as I appear now. (From the play *The Shape of Things*)

(2) Security Need, To prepare —To prepare her for survival after my suicide. (From the play *'Night Mother*)

(3) Body Need, To get —To get help for my family's survival from those who should step up now (From the movie *Cinderella Man*)

(4) Beauty Need, To enhance —To enhance this pitiful situation with beauty before I go mad (From the play *A Streetcar Named Desire*)

(5) Cognitive Need, To teach —To teach the boy the skills he needs before he starts training (From the movie *The Karate Kid*)

(6) Spiritual Need, To motivate —To motivate my sister to help me in this risky deed (From the play *Antigone*)

(7) Ultimate Fulfillment Need, To reveal —To reveal my secret life-affirming discovery to my proud daughter (From the play *Proof*)

(8) Ego Need, To regain —To regain my superior standing by undermining the aunt who is encroaching on my new territory (From the play *Hedda Gabler*)

Thoughts Chapter, Exercise on pages 74-75

Possible Victory Statement Answers for Discussion

Although the Victory Statement can vary slightly depending on the choices made by the actor, here are some suggested answers for the Creating a Victory Statement exercise.

(1) She will tell me she loves me as I am now.

(2) She will tell me she will manage without me.

(3) They will graciously give me money.

(4) He will be captivated by my transformation.

(5) He will thank me for my wise teaching methods.

(6) She will agree to help me, no matter the consequences.

(7) She will offer to help me further develop this masterful discovery.

(8) She will apologize for interfering in my marriage.

Actions Chapter, Exercise on pages 147-148

Answers for Identify the Weak Tactics:

(1) To *shout* only provides how the line is delivered with emotion and volume. It does not provide an action that implies an intended outcome.

(2) To *state* is too general a word, merely implying to say or to speak. We know your character is speaking, the character has a line to say. No choice of specific action has been provided.

(3) To *question* is obvious and generalized. The line is provided with a (?), so we already know it is a question. How is your character questioning?

(4) To *question* is a repeat of the previous beat, so already this is a weak choice for an action of a new beat. A new beat requires a new choice. Additionally, to question as an Action Tactic is not consistent with the actions provided by the lines throughout the beat. The first line the character provides is a question; however, as you read through the rest of the beat the character also exclaims, "Wow!" and confirms "I mean it." None of those are questions, so this would be a very poor choice for a beat tactic.

(5) To *ask* is too general. It is the same as listing the action, *to question*.

(6) To *whimper* provides an emotional delivery of a line, but does not provide an action that works toward a desired outcome.

(7) To *exclaim* means to yell or shout, providing an emotional delivery of the line, not an action used to get a result from the other.

(8) To *snarl* is yet another emotional delivery style of a line, not an action motivating someone else. Although a snarl may illicit a reaction from someone, it is not considered a strong choice of an Action Tactic because its primary meaning explains a style of delivery, and nothing else.

Notes

Plays and Screenplays Referenced

A Few Good Men, a screenplay by Aaron Sorkin

A Streetcar Named Desire, a play by Tennessee Williams

Agnes of God, a play by John Pielmeier

Antigone, a play by Sophocles

Art, a play by Yasmina Reza

Chariots of Fire, a screenplay by Colin Welland

Cinderella Man, a screenplay by Akiva Goldsman and Cliff Hollingsworth

Hedda Gabler, a play by Henrik Ibsen

Henry V, a play by William Shakespeare

Miss Julie, a play by August Strindberg

'Night Mother, a play by Marsha Norman

Proof, a play by David Auburn

Shrek, an animated film by William Steig & Ted Elliott

Something's Gotta Give, a screenplay by Nancy Meyers

The Big Chill, a screenplay by Lawrence Kasdan and Barbara Benedek

The Karate Kid, a screenplay by Robert Mark Kamen

The Shape of Things, a play by Neil Labute

The Taming of the Shrew, a play by William Shakespeare

Who's Afraid of Virginia Woolf?, a play by Edward Albee

Witness, a screenplay by Pamela Wallace, Earl W. Wallace, and William Kelley

CPSIA information can be obtained at www.ICGtesting.com
Printed in the USA
BVOW09s1653180815
413745BV00003B/10/P